MYSTERIOUS REALITIES
PERSPECTIVES FROM BEYOND
SPACETIME

by
Zachary Denman and Stephen Denman

INLIGHT MEDIA GROUP

ISBN 9798853683112

Copyright © 2023 by Zachary Denman and Stephen Denman

First published in 2023 by Inlight Media Group

All rights reserved. No part of this publication may be reproduced, distributed, or transmitted in any form or by any means, including photocopying, recording, or other electronic or mechanical methods, without the prior written permission of the publisher, except in the case of brief quotations embodied in critical reviews and certain other noncommercial uses permitted by copyright law.

Published by Inlight Media Group, United Kingdom

www.inlighttv.com

Cover design © 2023 by Zachary Denman and Stephen Denman

Cover artwork © 2023 by Zachary Denman and Stephen Denman

CONTENTS

PREFACE - 4
INTRODUCTION - 8
CHAPTER 1: THE GEOMAGNETIC LINES - 10
CHAPTER 2: ANCIENT ALIENS - 23
CHAPTER 3: THE SASQUATCH AND OTHER HAIRY HOMINIDS - 44
CHAPTER 4: AMERICAN INDIAN FOLKLORE - 56
CHAPTER 5: THE CIVILISATION OF TARTARIA - 68
CHAPTER 6: PRIMORDIAL GIANTS - 77
CHAPTER 7: HOLLOW EARTH ANOMALIES - 90
CHAPTER 8: BREAKAWAY CIVILISATIONS - 104
CHAPTER 9: PREHISTORIC WARFARE - 115
CHAPTER 10: SUPERNATURAL REALMS - 127
CHAPTER 11: BRITISH CRYPTIDS - 141
CHAPTER 12: ARTIFICIAL INTELLIGENCE - 153
CHAPTER 13: THE SPIRITUAL BATTLES - 167
CHAPTER 14: ASTRAL PROJECTION - 177

PREFACE

This book of Mysterious Realities, is inspired by the supernatural experiences of myself and my brother Stephen Denman. Because we have studied the "Unexplained Mysteries" throughout our lifetimes, we came to realise that there is much more beyond the frequencies and vibrations which resonate around us. There is so much history about the Planet Earth and Human Beings that has been censored and suppressed, or has simply has been forgotten. What we are taught from an early age is only a limited bandwidth of perception, and the version of actuality we have been given was only created to prevent us from knowing the truth. Therefore, we need to ask these questions. Why are we not presented with this concealed information in the mainstream media? Additionally, this knowledge is not taught in schools, colleges and universities? Why is that? The subjects we learn in these educational institutions often ignore the spiritual wonders of life, by simply relying on mundane facts and figures. While facts are of course important, we must also remember that we cannot completely ignore or reject subjective experiences and the etheric frequencies which are constantly present, even though we may not fully understand them.

We were brought up as three brothers in Chattenden, which is a village in Kent in South East England. I am the youngest, Stephen the eldest and Joel was the middle child. Even though all three of us had supernatural experiences, it was Stephen and I who discussed ours to a greater extent, as we grew up. Chattenden is surrounded by fields and there were meadows behind our house. The nearby village of Lower Upnor contained a lot of history from the

Medieval Period. We also lived close to Lodge Hill Military Camp, where many UFO sightings happened.

Our family lived in a terrace house at the top of Four Elms Hill, along the Main Road. Stephen had a room in the loft conversion and Joel and I shared the room below it. During his childhood, Stephen had many experiences of flying over the nearby villages close to Chattenden. Every aspect of his Astral Projections occurred just after he went to sleep and then he would find himself hovering over the back garden. Much of the time I experienced some very unusual reoccurring dreams about Giants and I often had visions about my past lives.

All three of us were deeply fascinated with the supernatural. Because the experiences we had occurred before the advent of the Internet, to further understand these supernatural based events, we therefore started to read the periodic magazine called 'The Unexplained: Mysteries Of Mind, Space, And Time' and unusual books that we found in Strood Library. Anything to do with UFO sightings, aliens or the supernatural, would excite us and then become topics of conversation. Both me and Stephen vividly recall talking about the story of the Phantom Cats, that were seen roaming around in the rural areas of Kent. We didn't observe the Phantom Cats unfortunately, but we were curious and wanted to find out more about the Cryptids.

During a windy Sunday evening, on the 12 October 1985, we became convinced that two men were watching us from across the dual carriageway. We thought they were the Men In Black or the Shadow People, that we had heard so much about. Stephen had read many books about UFO sightings, and therefore we started to believe the Men In Black were actually observing us. We closely watched the dark blue Talbot Alpine car as the two men sat in the front seats looking at us. The registration plate of the vehicle shimmered as the cars rushed past on the dual carriageway, obscuring the letters and numbers. Suddenly, there was a luminescent flash and the figures seemingly vanished from inside the car. Both of us talked about what had happened, and considered whether this event had actually occurred. This is one of many events that heightened our interest in conspiracy theories and the exploration of the unknown.

Around the back to our house there was a public footpath that led off from our back garden, past the playing fields, and into Towerhill Wood. There was a long term supernatural presence in this area because it had been used for witchcraft during the Medieval Period. Since our childhood we have discovered that there are many ley lines which run through that area of Lower Upnor. As children we explored some very unusual locations in this area of Kent. Such locations always felt very unsettling, although there was seemingly no logical explanation for any of it. On the 20 April 1986 we encountered a dark hazy Entity that we observed resting on a tree branch, next to the footpath in Towerhill Wood, which led down to Lower Upnor. The bizarre Entity appeared to be an opaque blob with red glowing eyes, that was silently watching us. It then dropped from the tree branch and started to run among the thorny bushes, making weird hissing and growling noises. We knew it wasn't physically real, but we also knew on some level that it was actually there. Hence, we still both ran off. The lifeform was some kind of etheric creature, which is why both of us had become worried. After escaping the woodland, we ran onto the playing fields. However, the creature didn't follow us.

Many incredible UFO sightings happened along the beaches and coastlines of the River Medway, near to Towerhill Wood, particularly when I was with Stephen. I would sense that supernatural activities were going on. Although something didn't feel right when the UFO sightings occurred, I was always intrigued by them. On the 17 June 1992 Stephen and I both observed a round metallic spacecraft at the back of the house in Chattenden. I remember how strange I felt after observing the spacecraft. Because of the supernatural events we experienced, there were times when both of us felt something was invisibly watching us.

The Internet has opened up a vast expanse of information that was almost impossible to obtain before it was invented on the 26 February 1991. Although disinformation is prevalent on the Internet, knowledge can now be fully researched and fact checked, just as we have done in this book. We cannot say with 100 percent certainty that all the subjects we have written about in this book have actually happened in the way they have been conveyed. However, we believe that it is very important to discuss these kinds of subjects as many individuals claim to have experienced supernatural events, just as we have. Furthermore, we believe that the educational conditioning which all of us have received, leads us away from developing our spirituality and understanding more about the knowledge of who we truly are. For Humanity to prosper and evolve, we have to always question the information we are given, as this will develop the spiritual self. If we reject the awakening of the self, this leads us towards a never ending cycle of dysfunctional thinking.

INTRODUCTION

We know that Secret Societies have censored and suppressed the knowledge of the Ancient World, by using subversion and manipulation since the prehistory of Human Beings. These kinds of restrictive controls occurred because multiple alien agendas seemingly became established on Planet Earth over many aeons. Hence, when it comes to supernatural incidents, UFO sightings and the "Unexplained Mysteries", most of these events have been censored or deleted. We must remember that if Humans made the effort to understand the frequencies in which they interact, we could then begin to comprehend how incredible the invisible existences are that resonate around us.

The result is that we are presented with an edited and managed perspective, which is constantly taught in schools, colleges and universities to program certain beliefs into the minds of Humans. When you actually study prehistory, it can bring amazing insights and therefore help an individual to develop the spiritual aspects of the self. Because of this same reason it can also enable you to use reflective thinking and help you connect with the self. By following the lies, they end up distorting our consciousness, which then restricts us. When this happens it can therefore make us completely unconscious to any other lies which have been told.

Within this book you will see the interconnection of all these subjects and how they resonate as different frequencies at the same time. You will see that Astral Projections, etheric lifeforms and other supernatural events, which you may have experienced yourself, are the keys to unlocking these censored revelations. This powerful knowledge can be used to question the condensed vibrations which seemingly define what we believe is real. We must remember that questioning everything around us is a healthy indication of a developing civilisation.

There have always been open minded individuals who want to learn about the knowledge which has been concealed on Planet Earth. Hence, It is our wish that by reading this book, you will realise that the narrative which has been presented by the Secret Societies is a complete delusion. More importantly however, is the fact that by unlocking the censored knowledge, we intend you will be able to enhance your own individual awareness.

Once enough individuals question the perspectives which have been presented to them, an effective political and spiritual awakening can happen. You must remember that the collective unconscious will always influence Human Beings. So if we continue to remain unaware, this allows the Secret Societies to influence and manipulate us. Therefore, information is our power and the only way to positively change is through the use of spiritual development.

CHAPTER 1: THE GEOMAGNETIC LINES

Over thousands of years, different tribal communities and civilisations have used ley lines as pathways to navigate across landscapes, but over many generations this information has been completely suppressed and somehow forgotten. The Romans were very well known to construct places of worship over Druid Groves and Druid Shrines, to honour the Roman Pantheon. When the Druids built in such locations, they ensured the surroundings were intersected by ley lines, which function as geomagnetic conduits that run through cities, towns and countries all over Planet Earth. Because these ley lines cannot be seen, most individuals are therefore unaware of them, but obviously they represent a lot more than we are told. What did the Humans from the past really know about ley lines? We know that during the Paleolithic, Mesolithic and Neolithic, most communities of Humans tended to roam and travel in a straight direction to guide themselves, by using mark points that were visible on the landscapes.

It is very common for UFO sightings to be observed above ley lines, so it is possible that these kinds of spacecraft are somehow tuning into the electromagnetic frequencies of Planet Earth. When the Druids ruled Ireland, the various Celtic Tribes defined the ley lines as the Línte Naofa (Sacred Lines). From prehistoric times the Chinese People defined the ley lines as the Lóng Xiàn (Dragon Lines). The spherical grid that is comprised of the ley lines, resonates around Planet Earth, where it produces a linear set of frequencies which pulsate in a single direction. Each of the frequencies then run from one landmark of historic importance to another, and sometimes the ley lines pass through certain natural formations along the way.

Within the United Kingdom, there are many ley lines which converge through London and the surrounding counties such as Kent and Essex. There are thousands of locations in the United Kingdom where the ley lines connect between historic landmarks and natural formations. Each of the ley lines functions like a conduit for the telluric currents of Planet Earth, which are the pulses of ground based electricity. This is the reason why so many stone circles, burial chambers and religious sites were constructed on the ley lines. Because the entire structure of Planet Earth has a powerful magnetic grid within it, this fact is of course largely ignored by most of Western Science.

Many of the intersecting ley lines were originally used as trade routes around the United Kingdom, and this information is described with quite some detail, in the book called The Old Straight Track, that was written by the English Antiquarian called Alfred Watkins. During 1972 to 1976, the English Esotericist known as John Frederick Carden Michell, researched the subject of ley lines, and realised they connected historic locations with different mark points. He showed how the ley lines additionally connect in numerous other places on Planet Earth and even resonate outwardly, into the Solar System and the stars.

Set out around London is a geometric pattern that includes triangles and alignments of ley lines that generate the prehistoric landscape which once defined parts of the Home Counties, before certain locations became integrated with Greater London. Did the British Druids really use the ley lines for more supernatural reasons? The first essential alignment in South East England is based on the important ley line which links Canterbury Cathedral in East Kent, and the site called Abbey Dore, in South Herefordshire. Can each of these alignments simply be a mere coincidence? None of this makes any sense unless a profound knowledge was shared and taught among prehistoric Humans.

A very significant ley line which is an important feature of London is a triangulated area that links the Royal Naval College at Greenwich, with Springpond Well on Wimbledon Common, and Boudiccas Mound on Hampstead Heath. Apparently this forms an equilateral triangle with the mark points of Boudiccas Mound on Hampstead Heath, the Tower of London in the City of London, and by the River Thames, and West Brompton Cemetery in South West London.

The energetic foundation of this second triangular area links the Tower of London, Southwark Cathedral, and the Palace of Westminster, that is also known as the Houses of Parliament, Westminster Abbey and the West Brompton Cemetery, plus a number of other key sites. There are many significant alignments or ley lines which link key locations across London, such as the alignment from the Royal Court in Westminster to the mound at Arnold Circus, which links the Royal Court in Westminster with Saint Martin to many buildings and ley lines. When the urban planning of London was developed, could the architects have known where to concisely position all these buildings unless they had some awareness of the ley lines?

Every single geomagnetic ley line has a distinctive electromagnetic start and end location. Many ley lines perfectly converge across London and other major cities such as Birmingham, Sheffield, Liverpool, Manchester, Newcastle, and within other urban areas in the United Kingdom. For generations the Druids of Ireland and Britain had used the ley lines for esoteric rituals and Ceremonial Magic, because they function as nexus areas for the telluric currents of electricity within the landscapes of Planet Earth. Such insights have been suppressed by the Elites and their Secret Societies because the ley lines are telluric currents of electricity which can help us to connect with our own spiritual potential.

Many individuals have seen different kinds of UFO and had paranormal experiences because there are intersecting ley lines, near to where they are. Whenever ley lines converge, it is believed that close proximity areas become supernatural zones. It is no accident that financial districts such as the City of London, are constructed in a location where numerous convergences of ley lines exist. Such vibrational resonances might sound fantastical but this is only because ley lines are not spoken about in Western Science. However, there are many organisations and businesses who believe they can enhance their own abundance by constructing their office buildings on ley lines. For thousands of years, the Chinese People have used the practice which has become known as Fēngshuǐ (Wind Water), and is a vibrational process that is effectively defined as Chinese Geomancy. These practices are based on positioning buildings on specific ley lines to create optimal wealth and prosperity for individuals, families, organisations and businesses.

The urban landscapes of London were built on geometric patterns that are comprised of ley lines. Across that city, as with many others, there are certain receptive Human Beings who know how to interact with the ley lines. However, most individuals on Planet Earth are unconscious and because they are unaware of the ley lines, their own frequencies can therefore be manipulated or controlled by someone or something else. When anyone looks at this knowledge about ley lines, it becomes clear how a long term inversion of the frequencies and vibrations that resonate around Planet Earth have deliberately been inverted for thousands of years, so the spiritual grid can be concealed from the public.

The longest and most well known ley line in England is Saint Michaels Line which runs from Cornwall, through Devon and elsewhere in South West England. It then extends all the way to Norfolk in East Anglia. Glastonbury Tor is one of the main points that Saint Michaels Line passes through, and the Summerland Meadows of the Somerset Levels in Central Somerset, that surround Glastonbury Tor, is a location where many kinds of bizarre supernatural events apparently happen. Other sites like Avebury Circle, in Central Wiltshire, and the Rollright Stones of North Western Oxfordshire, were major locations which the Irish Druids and the British Druids privately used. Many generations ago, those sites were actually Druid Groves and Druid Shrines. There are stories about King Arthur Pendragon visiting such locations, and even Jesus Christ apparently walked along the Saint Michael Line on his pilgrimage through Celtic Britain. An interesting aspect to Glastonbury Tor, is the near mythical presence of what became known as the Star Temple and the prehistoric Glastonbury Zodiac, which many ley lines converge upon. Did the Druids and Celtic Britons construct these formations to enhance the frequencies of the surrounding ley lines?

According to legend Saint Michaels Line represents the linear version of the blow which Saint Michael used to send the Devil into the Infernal Regions of the Lower Astral. Does this legend symbolise a possible electromagnetic polarity? Maybe this made the mark points an entrance into the Infernal Regions of the Lower Astral? Are these ley lines a major part of the Sacred Geometry that resonates around Planet Earth? These ley lines could actually be used to improve the mental health and spiritual awareness of Human Beings, but the ley lines have seemingly been inverted.

There is another ley line, which is known as the Saint Mary Line, that intersects the Saint Michael Line, at Saint Michaels Mount in Cornwall. The Saint Mary Line runs through seven monasteries from Ireland to Israel, and specifically begins in the Skellig Islands of County Kerry, in Southern Ireland. Saint Marys Line then passes through other significant locations such Mont Saint Michel in the Normandy Commune of France, extends through seven ley line points from Skellig Islands, and ending at the Stella Maris Monastery, which is situated on Mount Carmel in the city of Haifa, in Israel.

The name of the incredible Archangel Michael in the Latin is sometimes written as the phrase Quis Ut Deus? (Who Is Like God?). However, that name originates from the Hebrew Language, as the name Mikhael (Who Is Like The Creator). Does some connection exist between the name of the Archangel and certain ley lines in the United Kingdom?

When the First Heavenly Battle started, it was intended to be fought until the end of time, and according to Revelation 20:3 in the New Testament, the Devil or

Satan will be *"Cast"* into the *"Bottomless Pit"* within the Internal Regions of the Lower Astral, which is also a location that is known as Gehenna and Hell. These seven monasteries were perceived as safe havens from the Devil and his Demons, and Christians viewed themselves as the Holy Soldiers of the Lord Jesus Christ, who would have to fight against them. Everyone of them had the spiritual impulse to save the Human Soul from the subversive influences of the Devil and his Demons. Are there really links between the ley lines and the frequencies of good and evil?

The dictatorships of the Roman Empire were seemingly controlled by incessant evil and therefore, every aspect of true history had to be deliberately censored. The dictatorships of the Roman Empire intentionally silenced much of factual history so their own controls and dominance would continue. Hence, this is why the Roman Empire suppressed the Druids knowledge about ley lines. When the Roman Legions invaded Celtic Britain in 54 AD, the Roman General known as Julius Caesar, ordered that all of the Druid Priests should be eliminated in Celtic Britain. Wherefore, the Romans immediately set about the elimination of the Druids, which also included the destruction of the Druid Groves and Druid Shrines, which had been constructed on ley lines and mark points. Many of the standing stones were either demolished or reused. The Roman Empire knew that by destroying the Druidism which the Celtic Britons identified with, they could impose the patriarchal dominance of the Roman Empire. Once the Romans departed from Britain, churches, monasteries, castles, stately homes, mansions, and economic districts were built on these sites.

A major convergence point of ley lines is at Rudston in East Yorkshire, which is one of the most unusual and mystical locations in the United Kingdom, as it is the end mark point for many ley lines, and is a basic alignment of Britain. Where the ley lines intersect is where intense supernatural frequencies are known to be present.

The intersection seems to link with the prehistoric Rudston Monolith in the East Riding of Yorkshire, which is almost 26 feet high, and is where numerous hauntings occur. During the newer generations, numerous Druids used the Rudston Monolith for ritualism purposes, as it had been carved from Moor Grit Conglomerate in the Late Neolithic, and can absorb intense telluric currents of electricity.

Further ley lines radiate out from the Rudston Monolith to the ley line of Helvellyn Mountain, in Cumbria. Out to the Scilly Isles, like Saint Agnes, near to Cornwall. This ley line also connects Rudston to Prescelly or the Preseli Mountains of Pembrokeshire, in Western Wales. This location is where the enormous bluestones of Stonehenge were carved and then moved to Salisbury Plain in South Wiltshire, because the ley line of Pembroke in South Eastern Wales, and the ley line in Rudston, also connect to that area. How can all of these ley line connections be a mere coincidence?

Where there are stone circles and supernatural locations across Britain, is where you will also find an MOD Barracks of the British Army, or an RAF Base, or maybe a dual carriageway passing through ley lines. This means the frequencies of the stone circles have been disrupted or relocated, so the telluric currents which define the ley lines, have also been deviated or severed. If you look at UFO reports, it becomes clear that spacecraft are commonly observed nearby to Deep Underground Military Bases (DUMBs) or D1 Bases, which are often built close to these intersecting ley lines.

We have crop circles, which are cereal formations that display geometric patterns and unusual archetypal glyphs. Although many of the crop circles are fake, there are still many crop circles which are created by what appears to be Ultraterrestrials or Extraterrestrials. Some crop circles are beyond the comprehension of most Human Beings, and the consistent UFO activity which occurs above the crop circles of Wiltshire and Hampshire, in the United Kingdom, have revealed that crop circles are definitely real. There is an untapped potency to these prehistoric sites and therefore such crop circles are geometric formations which can help Human Beings to become more aware of their own spiritual development.

The construction of the M3 motorway began on the 14 October 1968 and was finally completed on the 22 June 1995. During the entire construction process is was likely decided to intersect the ley lines with the M3 motorway, so that it would cause energetic disruption. A relevant example of this, concerns the A33 Winchester Bypass which runs through Twyford Down, in Central Hampshire. The A33 Winchester Bypass was always perceived to be the most controversial section to have been constructed, after a series of protests were organised from the 16 March 1992 to the 5 August 1994.

For many generations the Chinese People have been very aware of how to locate the various Dragon Lines or Dragon Paths, because whenever a relative or close friend passed away, they would organise a walk of remembrance by carrying the decease relative or friend along the Sïde Dàolù (Dead Roads). Many ley lines in Mainland China actually converge were the Dàbái Jīnzìtǎ (Great White Pyramid) is located in the city of Xingping, midst the Shaanxi Province of North West China. Just as with that area of Eastern Asia, pendulum dowsing was also used in Mainland Europe to locate specific ley lines.

There seems to be so much history that has been deliberately censored and suppressed by the Secret Societies. When you observe this process, then you will be able to perceive a connection between their need to deviate the ley lines and the knowledge you have about their potency. The frequencies which define the 3D Holographic Reality of this Material Dimension, have been designed for you to participate within. Just as there is a grid formation of ley lines on Planet Earth, so there are meridians which cover the physical body, that function as energy points. The meditation practices of Hinduism define the meridians as the Chākraḥs (Wheels). Hence, by understanding how these ley lines and systems operate can help to give you a deeper understanding of yourself. Was it once possible for Humans to connect their own meridians to the grid of ley lines around Planet Earth?

According to the Celtic Folklore of Ireland, Wales and Scotland, there were Fairy Paths or the Sleachta Sióga (Fairy Passages). This kind of energetic conduit was a course taken by Fairies, which resonated in a straight direction between sites of traditional importance, such as the Fairy Forts (Dhúin Sióga), that were built in mountainous areas, hillsides, and the surrounding countryside, nearby to ley lines which resonate around various Neolithic Monuments.

Whenever a ley line has become a Fairy Path, it means the frequencies will be connected to a Fairy Ring. Much of Irish Folklore mentions how the Fairies who reside in the Astral Realms, would briefly appear inside the more condensed frequencies of the Fairy Ring, where they gathered to dance, as described by the famous Irish dramatist and poet known as William Butler Yeats, "...*The Fairies Dance In A Place Apart, Shaking Their Milk White Feet In A Ring...*" Although this concept is usually associated with Irish Folklore and Scottish Folklore, the Fairy Rings were also known to exist in Mainland Europe.

In some parts of Ireland, Britain, France and Germany there were Cosáin Sióg (Fairy Paths) and Tulacha Sióga (Fairy Mounds). These locations held tremendous importance for the Pagans, who deliberately adapted their building practices to ensure these kinds of ley lines were never obstructed. Across many areas in Northern Europe the artificially created long hillsides were the traditional homes of the Fairies, Elves, or Trolls, and were avoided by the Pagans. Different ley lines converged in such areas. The prehistoric Fairy Toot in Somerset, the Elf Howe Round Barrow in the East Riding of Yorkshire, and the long hillside of Beedon Barrow in West Berkshire, are examples of these structures.

Throughout Cornwall are electromagnetic strongholds of much Fairy Lore. According to the stories about the past, communities of Fairies were said to dance on Carn Gluze, near Saint Just on the Penwith Peninsula of South West Cornwall.

Midst the villages and towns of Ulster in Northern Ireland, and Connaught, in Western Ireland, the Irish

Celts have always known about where sickness or other misfortune has arisen because of the ley lines that have become Fairy Paths. This is because many houses were apparently constructed in the way of a Fairy Path, or in a contrary location to one, which then obstructed the Fairy Path, and this meant the frequencies of the ley line then became distorted.

All over Mainland Europe the subject of Fairy Lore has an extensive history. On the Jutland Peninsula of Northern Denmark there was a belief that Børfolk (Barrow People) dwelt in furrowed ground chambers, and were the descendants of Fallen Angels that had been cast out of Heaven. You have the the Elven People, from Germanic Folklore who apparently existed during the Medieval Period. Some aspects of Nordic Folklore mention the Alfebør (Wild Spirit Barrows) or the groupings of Elverbør (Elven Barrows), that were frequented by the Elverfolk (Wild Spirit People), who inhabited the North Jutland Region of Denmark.

Various ley lines converge across Mainland Europe, where they function as linear courses which the Soul Personalities of the deceased were supposed to use. Such conduits were known as the Leichenstrassen (Corpse Roads), that were generally believed to be given the same kind of relevance that Fairy Paths were given, and most likely shared the same origin. Within Germany and the Netherlands in particular, the Fairy Paths tended to be straight invisible conduits that were defined with a variety of names that include Geisterweg (Spirit Path), Sternenweg (Astral Path), and the Höllenweg (Infernal Path).

What is the connection between ley lines, natural geographic features and fortified buildings? From what is known, it would appear that most Humans did have a basic knowledge of ley lines and once upon a time numerous stories and legends were created as they were perceived with devotion. But where has the concealed information about ley lines gone?

CHAPTER 2: ANCIENT ALIENS

So are the aliens covertly living on Planet Earth? We are told the National Aeronautics and Space Administration (NASA) have never made contact or even communicated with Extraterrestrial Humanoids. With over a 450 billion stars in the Milky Way Galaxy, and over 130 billion galaxies in the entire Physical Universe, the probability of Extraterrestrials actually existing, is extremely probable and highly likely. We are given consistent lies and misinformation about the presence of Extraterrestrials that exist within the Milky Way Galaxy, but also through vast expanses in the Physical Universe. Therefore, it would seem that there is a secrecy and humans are disclosed the truth about the interstellar civilisations of Extraterrestrials, which are the normality beyond Planet Earth and the Solar System.

We only have to look at the last 75 years and examine the thousands of UFO sightings and physical accounts made by individuals in the United States of America. The phrase Unidentified Flying Object (UFO), first occurred when the famous American Aviator called Kenneth Albert Arnold observed a squadron of 9 metallic Flying Triangles on the 24 June 1947, over Mount Rainier, in the Cascade Range of the Pacific Northwest. The 9 metallic Flying Triangles had been flying over the Cascade Range of Mount Rainier National Park, in Washington State.
The case of the physicist called Robert Scott Lazar, who many also know as Bob Lazar, is utterly fascinating. He was interviewed on The Joe Rogan Experience, during the 21 June 2019, where Bob Lazar explained what happened when he was employed in the facility known as S-4 Base, which is located at Papoose Lake, near to the Papoose Range. According to Bob Lazar, the S-4

Base is located southward of Area 51, midst Lincoln County and the Great Basin Desert of South Eastern Nevada. During the interview Bob Lazar claims the S-4 Base definitely exists, and the below ground facilities are nearby the installation of Nellis Air Force Base, called Area 51, where numerous retrieved spacecraft and Extraterrestrials have been taken. Even though he has mentioned S-4 Base many times, the U.S. Army, U.S. Navy, U.S. Air Force, U.S. Marine Corp, U.S. Coast Guard and U.S. Space Force, which comprise the United States Armed Forces, and hence, the U.S. Defense Department, completely deny the existence of those subterranean facilities.

Bob Lazar claimed the S-4 Base consists of concealed metallic aircraft hangars which are covertly built into the side of the Sierra Nevada Mountains. He also mentioned that his job was to help with the reverse engineering of a particular kind of spacecraft, that had been selected from the other 9 metallic round spacecraft, which he alleged had been received from Extraterrestrial Humanoids.

The location called Area 51 is the name of a highly classified United States Air Force (USAF) facility within the Nevada Test and Training Range (NTTR), where a remote detachment is administered by Edwards Air Force Base. Even though that facility is located in Kern County, midst Southern California, which is over 328 miles or 529 KM from Area 51, it would seem that Muroc Army Airfield, which became Edwards Air Force Base, has very unusual connections with both the S-4 Base and Area 51. Because Edwards Air Force Base is the location where the Greada Treaty was signed on the 20 February 1954, between U.S. President David Dwight Eisenhower and the Rigelian Grays also known as the

Orion Grays. Could this be the reason why a remote detachment is administered by Edwards Air Force Base, at both the S-4 Base and Area 51? Across this expanse spacecraft are seen taking off and landing on a daily basis. What kinds of spacecraft are manufactured and tested in Area 51?

Because of the salt flats which surround this facility, the location was officially called Groom Lake and Homey Airport, as they are directly adjacent to the runways there. Any kind of research and occurrences which happened in Area 51 are classified as Sensitive Compartmented Information (SCI), which means no indications about what is really going on there, are ever presented as conveyed public knowledge.

Robert Scott Lazar was apparently used as a contractor by Edgerton, Germeshausen & Grier Incorporated (EG&G), and his employer was the United States Navy (USN), from the 20 April 1987 to the 30 June 1989. However, the corporation known as EG&G has stated that it had no records of Bob Lazar actually ever having been contracted by them. His supposed employment at a subsidiary of Nellis Air Force Base has also been discredited by skeptics, as well as by the United States Air Force (USAF). Has Bob Lazar been a truthful account of what has been going at the S-4 Base or not?

Bob Lazar explained how there is another set of frequencies and vibrations that are beyond this 3D Reality, but they resonate here on Planet Earth. Make of his information what you will but some of these spacecraft are beyond comprehension, because they defy the laws of physics as we know them. This means the kinds of subjects that have been taught as Western

Science in schools, colleges and universities, are partially or completely wrong.

Apart from the Roswell Incident, which occurred on the 8 July 1947, in Lincoln County, South Central New Mexico, there are many other accounts of crashed spacecraft. The Aztec UFO crash happened a few months later, on the 16 March 1948 in the Hart Canyon of North Western New Mexico. A disc shaped spacecraft apparently came hurtling out of the sky and crashed into the Hart Canyon, near to the city of Aztec, which is situated next to the Chihuahuan Desert, North Western New Mexico. According to the story, bodies of Extraterrestrial Humanoids were recovered, and some kind of applicable interstellar technologies were retrieved by the U.S. Air Force. Although the Aztec UFO crash is believed to be a possible hoax, no verifiable proof has ever confirmed it actually was.

The U.S. Navy filed patents for devices such as high temperature superconductors, gravitational wave generators, compact fusion reactors, Directed Energy Weapons (DEW), and electromagnetic field generators, which all sound like equipment from a Hollywood science fiction movie. However, these proponents are the components that were originally retrieved from crashed spacecraft, and were used to create interstellar travel. Why is the U.S. Navy designated with the role of dealing with the presence of both alien spacecraft and Extraterrestrials?

Many of the crashed spacecraft were originally reverse engineered by the United States Army Air Forces (USAAF), and then a lot of this process would be eventually carried out by the Defense Advanced Research Projects Agency (DARPA), the Office of Naval

Intelligence (ONI), the U.S. Air Force, and contractors employed by the U.S. Defense Department. Much of the reverse engineering has privately continued for over 75 years. Although considerable focus has been given to UFO crashes in the United States of America, there have been numerous UFO crashes in the Soviet Union of the Russian Federation, the Peoples Republic of China, and the Republic of India.

The video tape called 'The Secret KGB UFO Files' revealed an interesting UFO crash that occurred on the perimeter of Sverdlovsk, in Western Russia. Apparently the UFO crash happened on the 28 March 1969. The Rossiyskaya Politsiya (Russian Police) from the Ministry of Internal Affairs of the Russian Federation, investigated the UFO crash in Sverdlovsk. Once the investigation had been completed, designated contingents from the Sukhoputnyie Voyska, SV (Russian Ground Forces, RGF), covertly transported the UFO to the Sverdlovsk Army Barracks. However, this is only a single incident, but across the Soviet Union of the Russian Federation, there have been far more UFO crashes than in the United States of America.

The hybrid Unidentified Submersible Object (USO), claimed to be able to 'engineer the fabric' of the frequencies and vibrations around us, at the most fundamental level according to Doctor Salvatore Cezar Pais, who is the aerospace engineer and inventor from the United States of America, who is currently employed by the United States Space Force (USSF). He formerly worked at the Naval Air Station Patuxent River. Doctor Salvatore Cezar Pais believes that such aquatic spacecraft can instantly supersede the laws of physics. The official spokesperson for the Deputy Chief of Naval Operations for Information Warfare, Vice Admiral

Matthew Kohler, confirmed these kinds of spacecraft to be authentic, which means they do exist.

When the Vice Admiral Matthew Kohler, resigned on the 15 June 2020, he was replaced by Rear Admiral Jeffrey Trussler. Was this replacement instigated because the Secret Societies wanted to prepare the public for the next phase of the disclosure concerning alien spacecraft and Extraterrestrials, that would occur just over 12 months later? Many engineers and physicists have made it clear that they find the claims largely absurd, because they are not grounded in scientific fact. So what is going on? Does the U.S. Navy use a different kind of scientific knowledge that which is taught in conventional education syllabuses?

Much of Western Science has only seemingly been designed to consistently restrict and manipulate Human Consciousness. However, the concealed truth about the interstellar genetic and biological origins of Humans will not remain concealed for much longer.

Everything about the deceptive concept known as the 'Evolution Theory' which Charles Robert Darwin, widely proclaimed to be factual, is nothing but a farcical scientific delusion that has been taught in schools, colleges and universities for over 75 years, in an overt attempt to manipulate Human Consciousness. Hence, the presence of alien spacecraft and Extraterrestrials on Planet Earth, directly contradicts the entirely bogus Evolution Theory. Much of Western Science has only seemingly been designed to consistently restrict and manipulate Human Consciousness. However, the concealed truth about the interstellar genetic and biological origins of Humans will not remain concealed for much longer.

There has been an extensive history of UFO sightings in North America over 120 years ago. Early morning Saturday, the 17 April 1897, a very strange incident occurred in the small town of Aurora, in Wise County, North Texas. A cylinder shaped UFO that was metallic silver in colour, appeared suddenly in the sky above that urban area. It moved from the southward direction over Wise County, and continued northward, before the UFO supposedly crashed into a windmill. The incident was reported in the Dallas Morning News, on Monday, the 19 April 1897, where it was claimed the pilot of the UFO was 'not an inhabitant' from Planet Earth. Supposedly, the remains of the Extraterrestrial were buried in a grave at the Aurora Cemetery, and the remains of the metallic UFO were partially buried with the pilot. The other parts of the remnant UFO was said to have been dumped down a well next to the Aurora Cemetery.

The Phoenix Lights of Arizona that happened on the 13 March 1997, were a series of UFO sightings which lasted for over 3 hours, and were observed by thousands of Americans. Even though so many individuals witnessed the UFO sightings, very few of them managed to film or photograph the spacecraft. What became known as the Phoenix Lights.

Many radiant UFO vehicles of varying shapes and descriptions were seen by over 150,000 Americans between 7:30 PM and 10:30 PM MST. Throughout an expanse of about 302 miles or 486 KM, from the Nevada Border, numerous alien spacecraft were observed. They were then seen over the city of Phoenix, in Maricopa County. Just after this, each of the spacecraft flew over the city of Tucson, in Pima County, Southern Arizona. Some witnesses described observing what appeared to be a huge square UFO that contained 5 spherical, luminescent orbs. There were two distinct events which arose from this UFO sighting. The first was a triangular formation of spacecraft which passed over the city of Phoenix, and the second event happened on the 13 March 1997 at 7:55 PM MST, when a resident in the city of Henderson, in Clark County, South Eastern Nevada, reported seeing a large V shaped UFO travelling in a southeasterly direction. Then at around 8:15 PM, a former Police Officer in the Census Designated Place (CDP) known as Paulden, reported seeing a cluster of reddish orange looking spacecraft disappear over the southerly horizon.

Throughout all our history we have been given depictions of alien spacecraft, Ultraterrestrials and Extraterrestrials, in the petroglyphic artwork, scriptures and granite and marble carved statues. Huge amounts of prehistoric artwork from the Paleolithic, Mesolithic and Neolithic, depict various kinds of Unidentified Aerial Phenomena (UAP). For many tribal communities, the various kinds of Ultraterrestrials and Extraterrestrials were perceived as Deities, who had descended from the Heavens in their spacecraft. Even the hieroglyphs which are derived from the Phoenician Language, were designed as some kind of astronomical communication medium, that was based upon the shape of the constellations. Was the Phoenician Language influenced by the visitations of Ultraterrestrials or Extraterestrials? According to Irish Folklore, the Phoenician Language was actually created by the Druids. Were they influenced by aliens onboard interstellar spacecraft, to develop the Phoenician Language?

Various tribal communities on Planet Earth have always been fascinated with the Pleiades Star Cluster. These communities include the Cymric Welsh, Irish Celts, Scottish Celts, the Berber Arabs of North Africa, the Vedic Hindus and the Australian Aborigines. It would seem that the Pleiades Star Cluster is somehow connected with the different cultures on Planet Earth. Many aspects of Irish Mythology are concerned with the Tuatha Dé Danann (Tribe From The Bountiful Goddess), which reveals how these Irish Deities were actually Extraterrestrial who flew around on anti-gravity vessels. The prehistoric text describes how the Tuatha Dé Danann appeared over Ireland, by using their Longa Eitilte (Flying Ships), that were surrounded by expansive Scamailh Dorcha (Dark Clouds). From the stories of Irish Folklore which have been told about the Tuatha Dé Danann, it is not known whether or not they were from Neamh (Heaven) or the Domhan (Earth). Within the Holy Bible an indication is given about the otherworldly inception of the Lord Jesus Christ and the disciples, when it mentions.

"They Are Not Of The World, Even As I Am Not Of The World." - John 17:16.

In the Old Testament there is the story of Ezekiel Ben Buzi or Ezechiel Ben Buzi, where he describes a huge round carriage with wheels that descends from the sky, which is piloted by Extraterrestrials. This story from the Book of Ezekiel is covered very well in Chariots Of The Gods, that was written by Erich Anton Paul von Däniken, who is better known as Erich von Däniken. Because the book was published in 1968, it does show how the hypothesis called Ancient Astronaut Theory (AAT) has been given consideration for many years. Considering the Holy Bible has been rewritten many times, what does this story in the Book of Ezekiel actually mean?

Moving forward to World War 2, it is commonly known that the Führer (Leader) of National Socialist Germany, called Adolf Hitler, was interested with both Western Occultism and Eastern Occultism, and free energy technologies. What was unique about National Socialist Germany, is that it was the only dictatorship in history that based its principles on the concepts of Western Occultism.

The famous aeronautics scientist called Wernher Magnus Maximilian Freiherr von Braun, had been employed by the Drittes Reich (Third Empire), and whilst he was in German, Wernher von Braun developed the V2 rocket, which Adolf Hitler used to bomb cities like Brussel and other urban areas of Belgium, alongside London, in the United Kingdom. After the collapse of National Socialist Germany, Wernher von Braun left Europe and was given employment in the United States of America, under Operation Paperclip, that was a transference program created by the U.S. Department of the Army, that continued from the 20 June 1945 and ended on the 31 October 1959. Operation Paperclip was conducted by the Joint Intelligence Objectives Agency (JIOA), and was largely carried out by Special Agents from the Counter Intelligence Corps (CIC) of the U.S. Army.

Operation Paperclip was a highly covert transference program, which the U.S. Department of the Army planned and created, in which more than 1,600 German scientists, engineers, and technicians were initially taken from the former National Socialist Germany. Many of these personnel had been members of the Nazional Sozialistische Deutsche Arbeiter Partei, NSDAP (National Socialist German Workers Party, NSGWP).

After the transference program had ended, more than 250,000 scientists, technologists and engineers, from National Socialist Germany, had been settled in the United States of America, where they were deployed for the purpose of developing for Military Industrial Complex (MIC) under the guise of Operation Paperclip. Wernher von Braun then reinvented himself as the space flight advocate for the U.S. Federal Government. When the National Aeronautics and Space Administration (NASA) was formed out of the National Advisory Committee for Aeronautics, on the 29 July 1958, the internecine structure of NASA would be used for the covert development of highly advanced scientific endeavours. Whilst he was employed by NASA, as the Director of the Marshall Space Flight Center, from the 1 July 1960, Wernher von Braun also became the Space Architect of the Saturn 5 mission, which is the rocket that sent Neil Armstrong and the Apollo 11 crew to the Moon. We are told that Commander Neil Armstrong and Lunar Module Pilot, Buzz Aldrin, landed the Apollo Lunar Module Eagle on surface of the Moon during the 20 July 1969. Appparently on the 21 July, Neil Armstrong became the first officially accepted Human Being to stand on the Moon. Although, such an event is highly questionable, and very possibly never actually happened.

There are many NASA Astronauts such as Edgar Mitchell and Catherine Coleman, who is also known as Cady Coleman, and Doctor Brian O'Leary, that were part of the NASA Astronaut Group 6, who were also called the Excess Eleven or XS-11. All of them observed UFO activity while in outer space and their UFO sightings cannot be explained by NASA, or by anyone in the U.S. Defense Department. The former NASA aeronautic engineer known as Clark McClelland claims that he observed a 9 foot Extraterrestrial meeting with other

NASA Astronauts in the payloading bay onboard a Space Shuttle, during an orbital mission that happened began on the 5 June 1991. Clark McClelland had been employed by NASA at the John Franklin Kennedy Space Center or Kennedy Space Center (KSC), at the time he observed the huge looking Extraterrestrial. The location where Clark McClelland worked, is where numerous UFO sightings occur across Brevard County, which extends over the Merritt Peninsula of Eastern Florida.

According to the former NASA aeronautic engineer known as Clark McClelland, during the orbital mission of Space Transportation System 40 (STS-40), that was launched from Cape Canaveral, Eastern Florida, there appears to be the presence of Extraterrestrials in the Solar System. On the 5 June 1991 the orbiter called Space Shuttle Columbia (OV-102), was launched, and the mission then ended on the 14 June 1991. During the mission, a very unusual interaction occurred between NASA Astronauts and some kind of massive looking Extraterrestrial. Once the orbital mission had been completed, the Space Shuttle Columbia (OV-102) travelled back to Planet Earth, and landed at Edwards Air Force Base, midst Southern California. Both the NASA Astronauts who had met with the alien, said nothing about the interaction to anyone. The Space Shuttle Columbia (OV-102) landed on the exact same runway as the alien spacecraft of the Rigelian Grays had done, just before the Greada Treaty was established on the 20 February 1954, between U.S. President David Dwight Eisenhower and a designated Rigelian Gray.

Every U.S. President has to decide whether they disclose the existence of UFOs. Some are very vocal about it. When Donald John Trump became U.S.

President he created the United States Space Force (USSF). Was this to link the alleged the perceived gap between the breakaway civilisations and the far more consensus based scientific knowledge that has been promoted?

Over a 3 days period from the 26 December 1980 to the 28 December 1980, an incredible UFO sighting occurred in Rendlesham Forest, United Kingdom which is natural environment that ley lines course through, in a remote part of Suffolk. What became known as the Rendlesham Forest Incident occurred at the height of the Cold War between the Soviet Union of the Russian Federation, and the United States of America. A huge UFO sighting happened and became known as the British Roswell. Various kinds of unusual activity started happening in Rendlesham Forest, which is situated midst RAF Bentwaters and RAF Woodbridge. Both of these facilities had been seconded to the U.S. Air Force.

Lieutenant Colonel Charles Halt and many USAF Airmen observed what appeared to be orange coloured, luminescent UFOs moving around between the trees in Rendlesham Forest, crafts landing. A number of residents in the town phoned Suffolk Police because their household appliances had started to exhibit bizarre electrical anomalies. Sergeant James Penniston, who is an individual that many know as Jim Penniston, was with a contingent of USAF Airmen, that were stationed at RAF Woodbridge. Hence, they witnessed the alien spacecraft above and within Rendlesham Forest, before venturing into the wooded area on the 26 December 1980. Once there, Sergeant James Penniston and the other USAF Airmen observed some kind of alien spacecraft hovering and moving among the trees. After the encounter with the unusual alien spacecraft in

Rendlesham Forest, James Penniston, was able to recall a binary code and 5 sets of coordinates.

"During The Night I Was Often Wakening With Thoughts, Or Rather Images, Of Visions Of Ones And Zeros Running Through My Mind, My Mind's Eye." – Sergeant James Penniston, from the Rendlesham Forest Incident, 26 December 1980.

When he awoke from this trance-like perception, James Penniston found himself standing near the alien spacecraft. It began to glow once again, then ascended above the trees of Rendlesham Forest and vanished in an instant. The following day, James Penniston began to perceive images in his mind, which displayed thousands of ones and zeros. He did not know what to make of them, but James Penniston wrote them down in his notebook, along with drawings of the unusual glyphs.

Along with the help of the former Special Project Director at KMGH-TV on Channel 7, which is now called Digital 7 and Virtual 7, in Denver City, Colorado, the American investigative journalist and documentary film maker Linda Moulton Howe, and other experts, he discovered that the ones and zeros were actually binary code which translated to geographic locations in the USA and Egypt, Peru, China, Brasil and more. Additionally, other images that appeared in the minds of Sergeant James Penniston showed him longtitude and latitude coordinates, which even revealed the origin of the alien spacecraft which had transitioned into visibility on Planet Earth. The entry point longtitude and latitude coordinates for the alien spacecraft were displayed as Origin 52.0942532N 13.131269W. Lastly, a specific timeline origin of 8,100 AD was given for the year which the alien spacecraft had travelled from. Was the alien spacecraft piloted from the future?

What James Penniston observed intensely astounded him. Did he receive a message in binary code from Ultraterrestrials or Extraterrestrials? The binary code message apparently consisted of exact geographic coordinates for the Mayan Temple Complex at Caracol, which is in the Cayo District of Western Belize. Additionally, the coordinates were given for the city of Sedona, which is situated in both Coconino County and Yavapai County, Central Arizona. This area is where numerous UFO sightings occur. Why did the aliens give these coordinates to James Penniston? Are the coordinates somehow linked to the ley lines which converge in those geographic locations?

So many unusual events happened during the Rendlesham Forest Incident, because the UFO sightings which occurred in this part of Suffolk, were somehow connected with the nearby convergent ley lines, that course throughout Rendlesham Forest and other locations in East Anglia. The reason for the UFO activity was because certain armoured depots at RAF Bentwaters and RAF Woodbridge, had been constructed either side of Rendlesham Forest, for the purpose of storing nuclear weaponry. Rendlesham Forest is still full of the stories to this day, so there is no doubt a major ley line convergence in this location.

Then of course we have the Roswell Incident which happened on the 8 July 1947, where a weather balloon from the U.S. Air Force apparently crashed. But there are to many anomalies with the Roswell Incident, for it to simply have been a weather balloon. Whilst the Roswell Incident was taking place, the covert transference program known as Operation Paperclip was going on. Was the Roswell Incident used by the United States Army Air Forces (USAAF) to retrieve advanced Occult Technology? Were the remnants of the alien spacecraft from the Roswell Incident used to construct some of the first anti-gravity devices? Were a number of Ultraterrestrials or Extraterrestrials actually retrieved from the crashed UFO? During the Roswell Incident what became known as Operation Paperclip, was taking place in the United States of America. Operation Paperclip was established by the U.S. Federal Government, so they could employ scientists and technologists from National Socialist Germany.

Many of the scientists and technologists were deployed to Wright Field, which eventually became known as Wright Patterson Air Force Base (WPAFB). This facility is situated is a location where numerous UFO sightings occur. The remnants of the alien spacecraft and occupants from the Roswell Incident were transported to Roswell Army Air Field (RAAF) in Central New Mexico, and were then moved to Fort Worth in North Eastern Texas, and were then flown to Wright Field, which is a location that eventually became known as Wright Patterson Air Force Base (WPAFB). Why were scientists and technologists really deployed there? Does a connection exist between the Roswell Incident and Operation Paperclip? We must remember that numerous other retrieved alien spacecraft, Extraterrestrials, were covertly transported to Wright Patterson Air Force Base. The aliens that were placed there, were also interviewed. Hence, this means transcripts of the conversations with the different Extraterrestrials, have been recorded and safely kept away from the public. During the 23 December 1947, the transistor radio was successfully produced. Such transistor radios used the first ever circuit boards. There was boom in ongoing technological developments, because deductive reasoning had been implemented to manufacture new components and gadgets from the alien spacecraft which crashed during the Roswell Incident.

There is some evidence to suggest that U.S. President David Dwight Eisenhower met with malevolent Extraterrestrial Humanoids on the 20 February 1954 and signed what became known as the Greada Treaty, which apparently was an interstellar agreement that U.S. President Eisenhower made with the Rigelian Grays, in exchange for advanced Occult Technology. As part of the terms and conditions in the Greada Treaty these kinds of malevolent aliens would only be allowed to carry out experiments on livestock, minerals and certain listed Americans. This historical story cannot be proven and therefore whatever happened at Edwards Air Force Base, in Southern California, will never be known. Maybe some of the X Files episodes with FBI Special Agents Fox Mulder and Dana Scully, were informing the public about these kinds of events in a fictional way.

We can see that any ongoing retrieval of crashed UFO vehicles, whether they occur in the United States, Mainland Europe, or in the Soviet Union of the Russian Federation Russia and the Peoples Republic of China, seem to eventually result in the Military Industrial Complex (MIC) becoming even more powerful. Hence, if this is the case, then it is highly likely that advanced Occult Technology has been successfully reverse engineered, and some kind of covert interstellar faction has taken over the Solar System. We need to understand that if the Roswell Incident actually happened on the 8 July 1947, and the Greada Treaty did occur during the 20 February 1954, were various kinds of Occult Technology obtained from these events, by using the process of reverse engineering? This specific technical method would have been used, to discern how the onboard gadgets, devices and equipment of spacecraft function. Only by doing this, would the breakaway civilisations have been able to become fully achievable. Hence, we need to ask why is there such a vast divide between the scientific endeavours of Humans who exist in the 3D Holographic Reality of this Material Dimension, and the Humans which covertly established the different breakaway civilisations? Are their civilisations of Ultraterrestrials and Extraterrestrials who consistently interact with the breakaway civilisations?

If certain kinds of Ultraterrestrials or Extraterrestrials were already living among us, would anyone even realise they here? Do we know everything about the different cultures in our neighbourhoods? And if the Rigelian Grays have the ability to manufacture interstellar spacecraft or advanced Occult Technology like so many have observed, then the Rigelian Grays would probably have the ability to conceal themselves whenever they wanted to mingle among Humans.

What is crucial to mention here is that Humans only perceive 2 percent of the Visible Light Spectrum, which is a very narrow bandwidth of perception. Many resonant lifeforms probably do exist in the 98 percent of the Visible Light Spectrum that Humans cannot naturally perceive. Within a networking device such as a router or computer hardware device like a modem, which transmits a wireless signal, does anybody see the actual signal going into that computer? Do any Humans actually perceive the conversations we have on telephones or a mobile phones, floating in the airwaves?

One of the most supernatural areas on Planet Earth, is a location called Skinwalker Ranch, which is also known as Sherman Ranch. Like many other parts of Uintah County, in North Eastern Utah, as with the rest of the Mountain West Region in the Western United States, huge amounts of UFO and paranormal activity seem to occur on a regular basis. The fields around the Skinwalker Ranch, are where numerous UFO sightings and the presence of various Astral Spirits and Shadow People, have been observed. This area of North Eastern Utah was once populated by the Yuta Indians, who are likewise called Yutah Indians and the Núchiu (People). Because the Navajo Indians, or the Diné Indians or Naabeehó Indians, were more aggressive than the Yutah Indians, they captured some of them and used them as slaves. When a territorial dispute occurred on the 23 June 1865, and the Yutah Indians fought back, the Navajo Indians decided to curse North Eastern Utah, and unleashed the Skinwalkers.

Upon of the rocks in North Eastern Utah, there are petroglyphic diagrams of what became known as the Hatsís Hóósjdígí (Shape Changer) and the Inoolinígí Hóósjdígí (Shape Changer), the Hatsís Néizgizígí (Shape Changer) and the Inoolinígí Néizgizígí (Shape Changer), which date back to over 4,500 BC. This means the Skinwalkers obviously existed in North Eastern Utah long before the Navajo Indians cursed that area. Maybe there are frequencies and telluric currents, which resonate from the ley lines around the Skinwalker Ranch, that open dimensional portals. According to many of Navajo Indians the potency of the Akágí Joogááłígí (Skin Walker) meant it could transform into any different kind of animal, simply by using focused psychic volition. Once the Navajo Indian who has become a Skin Walker, fully transforms, if a Human gazes upon them, the Skin Walker can then absorb themselves into the body of the observer to influence their minds and actions. This is why such kinds of Ceremonial Magic were so popular among the Navajo Indians.

This kind of research does reveal how intricate and bizarre the subject of Unidentified Aerial Phenomena (UAP), UFO sightings, Ultraterrestrials and Extraterrestrials, really are. From the perspective of most rational thinking individuals, the various UFO stories are dubious, as they are very difficult to prove and validate. Ultimately, each of these events is based on the subjective and personal experience of the experiencer. Hence, unless the UFO sightings are filmed or photographed, especially in this day and age with either professional video cameras, or with mobile phone cameras and Closed Circuit Television (CCTV) cameras, the existence of alien spacecraft, Ultraterrestrials and Extraterrestrials, is very hard to prove. But when you read about identical UFO stories in different cultures around Planet Earth, it therefore becomes a futile exercise to keep saying that alien spacecraft, Ultraterrestrials and Extraterrestrials are imaginary concepts.

The U.S. Air Force recorded around 12,564 reports of UFO sightings under Project Blue Book, just for the United States of America, between the 8 March 1952 to its termination on the 17 December 1969. Hence, these UFO sightings cannot just be hallucinations or the products of imaginative minds. The U.S. Federal Government also declassified around 1,584 UFO reports, from the Advanced Aerospace Threat

Identification Program (AATIP), that was created by the U.S Defense Department, and which lasted from the 14 December 2007 to the 31 December 2012

So do aliens exists? In our estimable opinion, yes, they do. However, the majority of Humans could not emotionally and psychologically cope with the idea of Extraterrestrials revealing themselves to the public. Can you imagine what would happen if aliens really did appear on a News Channel? What would occur if Humans were given the Occult Technology and interstellar knowledge by the aliens? Such an event can never happen, because how would Humans be able to spiritually develop, if aspects of Occult Technology were shared with us? The various civilisations of Extraterrestrials would be viewed as superior incarnations, and therefore such an event would become adverse to the spiritual development of Humans. From knowing this, we should accept that the future we are moving into means the old mind patterns which many identify with during their lifetimes, will diminish. Once this occurs, Humans can start to embrace far more supernal perspectives. The different kinds of more benevolent Extraterrestrials will always invisibly observe Humans, and such lifeforms will continue to remain concealed, until the spiritual development of Humans has increased and we embrace the wholeness of our potential.

CHAPTER 3: THE SASQUATCH AND OTHER HAIRY HOMINIDS

The bipedal lifeform called the Sasquatch or Bigfoot started to be regularly observed from the 15 February 1803, when a trapper known as Cluey Derrick Koperland, observed a Sasquatch or Bigfoot that was roaming across Mount Katahdin, which is located in Piscataquis County. Apparently other Sasquatches had been seen in other parts of Central Maine and elsewhere in the North Eastern United States. Most of these bipedal lifeforms are sighted in Canada and the United States of America. But they have also been seen in other remote locations on Planet Earth. There are elusive lifeforms known as the Snegovik (Snowman) and the Yeren, which inhabit the countryside in the Russian Federation and the Peoples Republic of China. Other comparable bipeds exist, which are known as the Yowie, that inhabits rural areas in the Commonwealth of Australia and the Yeti, which lives in remote locations across the Tibet Autonomous Region and Nepal.

The oldest account of Bigfoot was recorded in 986 AD by the Norseman who became a famous explorer and navigator. His name was Leif Erikson, and he became very famous. For many Icelanders, he was also historically known as Leiv Eiriksson, Leif Ericson and Leif Eiricsson. Both he and other Icelandic Vikings landed in the New World, where they explored a geographic expanse which the Icelandic Vikings called Vinland. Some of the Icelandic Vikings also called the landmass Winland or Vineland. That specific area of countryside is now called the Meadows Cove of Newfoundland and Labrador, in Eastern Canada. Many times, the Icelandic Norsemen wrote about huge manlike lifeforms that were 'horribly ugly' creatures with black eyes.

During the Early Medieval Period, the famous Norseman known as Leif Erikson and other Icelandic Vikings, sailed across the North Atlantic Ocean. After they moored their ships at Meadows Cove of Newfoundland and Labrador, in Eastern Canada, Leif Erikson and the other Icelandic Vikings observed a massive looking bristly lifeform who towered over them. Others were also observed, and because of their appearances, Leif Erikson called the creatures Loethinn Thursar (Hairy Giants) and Skraelingjar (Dried Covering Foreigners). Such lifeforms are known today as the Sasquatches or Bigfoots. Although the encounters of Leif Erikson and the other Icelandic Vikings represent the earliest recorded story about the Sasquatches or Bigfoots, it is likely that the Mikmaq Indians, who were also known as the Beothuk Indians or Beothuck Indians, had encountered the Sasquatches in many parts of Newfoundland. Because the Inuit Eskimo Indians have inhabited Labrador for many generations, it is probable that some of them have also observed the creatures. According to Leif Erikson the huge "Hairy Men" would appear from nowhere and exuded an odour, whilst the creatures would shriek loudly. It should be noted that Leif Erikson and the other Icelandic Vikings clearly describe observing large manlike lifeforms that were foul smelling and very loud, which means they had no connection with the local First Nations Canadian Indians.

Apparently, Leif Erikson had numerous sightings of the "Hairy Men" before he departed from Vinland. Many of the Sasquatches have been seen on Prince Edward Island and across Northern Quebec, in Eastern Canada.

Some aspects of Icelandic Folklore, defined the Sasquatches as the Loethinn Lýethr (Hairy People). The Icelandic Vikings called the Sasquatch, the Loethinn Thursar (Hairy Giants) and Skraelingjar (Dried Covering Foreigners), Even though the Norsemen were bristly and large, and weaved their hair and beards, they remarked on the bristly looking bodies of the Sasquatches or Bigfoots. Was this because the Norsemen observed that such lifeforms were much hairier than them?

Just as with the rural areas of Canada, there are many locations in the United States of America, where gatherings of Sasquatches invisibly exist. The renowned prospector and backwoodsman, Albert Ostman claimed that he spent around a week with a Bigfoot family near Toba Inlet, British Columbia on the 18 June 1924. The legends of the Sasquatch or Bigfoot started to become known to Americans, from the summer of 1924 and onwards. Because so many sightings of the Sasquatch or Bigfoot have occurred, the massive bipedal lifeform therefore became a definable Cryptid. Usually described to be an enormous bipedal creature usually standing between 8 feet to 10 feet in height.

The Patterson Gimlin Film (PGF) was created on the 20 October 1967, in Bluff Creek, California, by filmmakers Roger Patterson and Robert Gimlin. What they filmed appears to be some huge female Sasquatch or Bigfoot. This footage is most definitely questionable. But the rivers round Bluff Creek within the National Forest of Del Norte County and Humboldt County are known to areas where supernatural activity occurs.

According to the perspective of the Dakota Medicine Man, known as Raymond Owen *"They Exist In Another*

Dimension From Us, But Can Appear In This Dimension Whenever They Have A Reason To." This quote is from the book "*In The Spirit Of Crazy Horse*" that Peter Mathiessen wrote in 1983. Sasquatches or Bigfoots are found in remotes part of America and Canada and it wouldn't be hard for such Hairy Hominids to conceal themselves in the remote forested areas.

Many of the Cherokee Indians have existed for generations with a knowledge of the Sasquatch or Bigfoot. They have always defined the bipedal lifeforms as the Yeahoh (Hairy Giants) and the Yuwanaoh (Hairy Giants), who were brought to Planet Earth by the Nokwsi Aniyvwi (Star People) during the prehistoric times. Additionally, the settlements of the Cherokee Indian believed they were the Utanayvwi (Giant People), which similarly became known as the Utanayvwi (Giant People). From the perspective of the Cherokee Indians, such lifeforms were connected with the Dijvysdi Dejiyu (Light Planes), that was an etheric location they sometimes defined as the Ulogilv Dejiyu (Cloud Planes), the Adelvunegv Dejiyu (Silver Planes) and the Usgosdi Dejiyu (Bright Planes).

On the 28 October 1965, the Sasquatch or Bigfoot was added to Index 1 of the Krasnaya Kniga (Red Book), that was officially called the Russkaya Krasnaya Dannyie Kniga (Russian Red Data Book). Inside this incredible document was the Vymirayushchikh Raznovidnostey Spisok (Endangered Species Register), that was reviewed every 12 months, and then published by the Gosudarstvennaya Dobycha Geologicheskaya Sluzhba (State Mining and Geological Service), in the Soviet Union of the Russian Federation. The countries of France and Germany then followed suit on the 12 June 1967, and followed the same monitoring process.

What is even more amazing is how the County Commissioner known as Conrad Lundy, of Skamania County, in Southern Washington State, passed Bigfoot Ordinance No. 69-01, on the 1 April 1969, declaring *"Any Willful, Wanton Slaying Of Such Creatures Shall Be Deemed A Felony"* and subject to fine or imprisonment. Because this legislation was passed on the 1 April 1969, the County Commissioner known as Conrad Lundy, said at the time, *"This Is Not An April's Fools Day Joke, There Is Reason To Believe Such An Animal Exists."*

Even though many individuals believe the Sasquatch does not exist, so what was the reason for the Russian Federation, the French Republic and the Federal Republic of Germany putting the bipedal lifeform on an endangered species list? Besides the strange footprints and trail marks over the years.

There is a connection of a type of Sasquatch or Bigfoot, Yeren, the Yowie, and the Yeti, have all been extensively recorded and documented. Once you look into the American Indians, the artwork, the stories and their prehistoric culture, it becomes clear that the Sasquatches are not fictional, and this is why they became an integral part of American Indian Folklore.

During the 14 October 1887 Edward Herman Wyatt encountered a Native American from the Yurok Tribe, who reside in Humboldt County and elsewhere in Northern California. The communities of Yurok Indians are likewise known as the Yurúkvarar and Yurukyara. According to the story, he was carrying a plate of meat. Edward was curious to where the Native American was taking the food. He asked the Yurok Indian and he told

Edward to follow him. They reached a cavernous opening in the cliff face of a place called Pierce Mountain. Edward Herman Wyatt then observed a massive Humanoid who was covered in hair, sitting down on the ground. The Yurok Indian gave the plate of meat to the Sasquatch, who was named "Crazy Bear", as he had supposedly been brought to the forested areas "*From The Stars*" by the Star Brothers.

According to the Yurok Indian, the Sasquatch or Bigfoot had been carried onboard a UFO that had the appearance of the Moon. The alien spacecraft had descended from the stars and then ejected Sasquatches or Bigfoots into the wooded areas of North Western California. The round glowing spacecraft was reportedly piloted by Extraterrestrials who appeared to have been extremely tall, and who had white complexions and long blonde hair. The starfaring Extraterrestrials would always wave at the Yurok Indians as they transported the Sasquatches onto the remote territories of the Yurok Indians, who inhabited areas next to the Klamath River in North California, and South Oregon, from where it flowed into the Pacific Ocean.

Another intriguing account which links the Sasquatches with UFO sightings, occurred during the 15 September 1888, when a meeting took place between European Americans who were cattle ranchers and a group of Maidu Indians, next to the Sacramento River in Northern California. Apparently, there had been numerous encounters which the Maidu Indians had collectively observed. They had seen various Sasquatches appear whenever some kind of Unidentified Aerial Phenomena (UAP) became apparent near to the Sacramento River. According to the Maidu Indians, many alien spacecraft were also seen on different occasions over the

Mendocino National Forest of the Coastal Mountain Range, and by the banks of the Feather River, which is a tributary of the Sacramento River. Some of the Maidu Indians had likewise observed alien spacecraft over the American River of the Central Sierra Nevada Mountains. The cattle ranchers learned that the Maidu Indians had observed what they described as "*Three Crazy Bears*" who had descended from the "*Starry Heavens*" in a "*Small Glowing Moon*". After this happened, the Sasquatches would be left in the wooded area, before the alien spacecraft took off again.

The renowned lumberjack, prospector and woodsman, Albert Ostman, revealed on the 6 February 1957, that he had been abducted by a Sasquatch, whilst he had been on vacation nearby Toba Inlet, which is located along the British Columbia Coast of Western Canada, during the 18 June 1924. Albert was resting, when suddenly he was carried off by a Sasquatch whilst he was in his sleeping bag. Apparently the Sasquatch then walked across the countryside for 3 hours, and then Albert was placed on a plateaued where he observed that a family of four Sasquatches that were sitting around him. From what Albert Ostman mentioned, he stayed with the Sasquatches for 6 days, before escaping from them. Whether the story of Albert Ostman is true or not cannot be verified, but the authenticity of the story has been open to debate for many years. Are the communities of Sasquatches are interdimensional lifeforms, who can shift from existing in the 3D Holographic Reality of this Material Dimension, to then suddenly vanishing whenever they want to?

Much of what has been written about, concerning the behaviour of the Sasquatches or Bigfoots, do indicate there is something very supernatural about them.

Whenever the Sasquatches are seen in locations such as the Umatilla National Forest, in the Blue Mountains of North East Oregon and South East Washington, they appear to flicker into visibility and then suddenly vanish. Additionally, there are other habitations which the Sasquatches apparently use for the same purpose, and these include the Klamath National Forest in the Cascade Range and Klamath Mountains in Northern California, this could explain why Sasquatches will leave footprint tracks which then suddenly disappear, or why no footprints are observed when the Sasquatches have been seen walking over muddy ground in forested areas. Many individuals have seen how the Sasquatches can slow their own vibrations, to become condensed and observable. This indicates that perhaps the Sasquatches are able to psychically shift their frequencies, and move across vast distances in Canada and the United States of America.

Hence, it becomes clear that perhaps the Sasquatches have a subterranean civilisation that is possibly located in the Hollow Earth. They seem to want to be left alone, and because Sasquatches do not trust Human Beings, most of them avoid any contact with the Western World. Everyone of the Sasquatches are extremely psychic and telepathic. Because of this the Sasquatches can instantly shift their own frequencies and disappear. They seem to be using geomagnetic leylines to traverse huge distances, before appearing once again in a new rural area. Many of the reports about the Sasquatches reveal that the bipedal lifeform seemingly travel onboard UFOs, and the Extraterrestrials which guide the spacecraft then place the Sasquatches into remote forested areas. So maybe there is truth when the Yurok Indians spoke of these Hairy Humanoids coming from a UFO that looked like the Moon.

Although this is only a theory, we need to consider the possibility that Sasquatches or Bigfoots can rapidly traverse across North America, by using their own psychic abilities, as they have the potency to connect with the geomagnetic leylines and vortices, this would explain why the Sasquatches are observed for a certain amount of time in specific locations, and then no sightings will occur for months on end. The gatherings of Sasquatches seem to use the Earths subterranean passageways and therefore is it possible for the Sasquatches are linked to the Hollow Earth?

Alongside the legends of the Sasquatch or Bigfoot, we have the Yeti, which is a lifeform that is likewise known as the Abominable Snowman. These kinds of creatures are large, fuzzy covered Humanoids that apparently inhabit cavernous openings in the Himalayan Mountains of Nepal. The word 'Yeti' comes from the Tibetan Language, and means 'Rocky Place Bear'.

During the 15 August 1921, the Irish British Soldier called Lieutenant Colonel Charles Kenneth, led an Everest Expedition. He was accompanied by the British Journalist called Henry Newman, who interviewed the Tibetan Sherpas, that told him stories about the Metoh Kangmi, which means Human Bear Snowman.

Different aspects of Russian Folklore have always defined the Yeti with the name Chuchuna, which is a bipedal lifeform that inhabits Siberia and other areas of Eastern Russia, where there are very few habitations of the Turkic Peoples and Slavic Russians. This bulky muscular Humanoid has been described as standing 8 to 10 feet tall and is covered with dark reddish fuzzy hair. According to the native accounts from the nomadic

Yakuts or Sakha from the Sakha Republic of Eastern Russia. The unusual Chuchuna has always been described as very muscular, and seems to have features which are similar to those which physically define the Neanderthals. With psychical ease, the Chuchuna seem to use teleportation so they can travel large distances. From most of the accounts which concern the Sasquatches or Bigfoots, they appear to have a tremendous reverence for the ecosystems around them, whilst the Yeti seems to have a different perspective about their environments, because they are Humanoids who live in the icebound wastelands of the Himalayan Mountains.

Stories about the Yeren are very widespread across the Peoples Republic of China, especially within the Shennongjia Forestry District of the Hubei Province, in Central China. Indeed, the Yeren have become a very important aspect of Chinese Folklore over many generations. The elusive Yowie of Australia has always been seen perceived as a lifeform of importance by the different Aboriginal Australians. Even though no evidence has ever been able to prove there is any genetic connection between these elusive Humanoids, they do look physically very similar. Such creatures always seem to reflect the environments they inhabit. Yowie inhabits the vast expanses of the Australian Outback. They apparently reside in numerous locations across Queensland, where the Yowie is known as the Quinkin and the Joogabinna. Across parts of New South Wales the communities of Humanoids are called the Ghindaring and the Jurrawarra by the Aboriginal Australians. The same kind of Humanoids are known to also inhabit Mount Bartle Frere, in North Eastern Queensland. Some of the Aboriginal Australians similarly define the creatures as the Myngawin, the

Puttikan, the Doolaga, the Gulaga and the Thoolagal. Most of these bipedal lifeforms have been observed in South Australia, Queensland and New South Wales.

Do the Sasquatches or Bigfoots have some kind of genetic connection with certain kinds of Mammal? The nearest version of the Sasquatch or Bigfoot in the South Eastern United States, is called the Skunk Ape, which is also known as the Florida Bigfoot and Swamp Ape. From the descriptions that have been given, it does appear that the Skunk Ape has some comparable features with the Sasquatches or Bigfoots. However, the Skunk Ape is very small, has a slim physique and only inhabits the swamps and marshes of Florida. The Sasquatch or Bigfoot is a very different type of Hairy Humanoid, because the way the Sasquatch walks is nothing like the way a Skunk Ape will walk. Everyone who has observed a Sasquatch or Bigfoot, mentions that such lifeforms physically massive looking, bristly Humanoids. These bipedal creatures normally have faces which have similar features to those of Human Beings. Some of the Sasquatches have also been described as having faces that are similar to a Canine or an Ursid, which is a taxonomic category for Bears. Do the features of such lifeforms indicate that different kinds of Sasquatches exist across the wildernesses of North America?

Obviously digital technologies and video cameras, to gather authentic film footage and photographs as evidence which could be used to confirm that the Sasquatch, the Bigfoot, the Yeti, the Yowie, and Yeren, really do exist. We know that such lifeforms deeply mistrust Human Beings and deliberately stay away from us. Hence, locations such as the Umatilla National Forest, in the Blue Mountains of North East Oregon and

South East Washington, have become remote habitations for the Sasquatches to conceal themselves within. Other residencies which the Sasquatches use include the Klamath National Forest, in the Cascade Range and the Klamath Mountains of Siskiyou County, in Northern California, and Jackson County in South Oregon. Do these bipedal lifeforms even originate from the ecosystems which they have made into their own residencies?

So do the Sasquatches exist in North America? Does the Yeren exist in the Soviet Union of the Russian Federation and the Peoples Republic of China? Does the Yowie exist in Australia? Does the Yeti exist in the Tibet? If you sighted these lifeforms in some remote countryside area, would you want to get your camera out and take photographs of these creatures? Such bipedal lifeforms are certainly very intelligent, but do not particularly like or trust Humans. They are known to be very aggressive and for good reason. There are so many stories concerning the Sasquatch, the Bigfoot, the Yeti, the Yowie, and Yeren, it does seem likely that such bipedal lifeforms actually do exist.

CHAPTER 4: AMERICAN INDIAN FOLKLORE

For many aeons the American Indian Tribes have maintained spiritual connections with different Ultraterrestrials and Extraterrestrials. We have always been told that Native Americans were individuals who apparently rode on horses, and would use Smoke Dances, and Earth Lodges, which to some extent is true. From the historical perspective, the various American Indian Tribes also used Spirit Lodges, Rain Dances, Sweat Lodges, spears, tipis, wickiups, and smoke signals, as important aspects of their cultural development. However, the Native Americans were actually far more focused on their relationship with the Physical Universe, and therefore by using these practices they emphasised the relevance the ecosystems of the Great Spirit Mother. Hence, the lives of the American Indians centered on respecting the landscapes and wildlife of the North American Continent, because for them, every aspect of Mother Nature was an important part of their own spiritual development. Because of the collective perspectives which the American Indians held and cherished, the knowledge they convey is utterly profound and very supernatural.

The Sugpiaq, who are the First Nations Canadian Indians who are likewise known as the Pacific Eskimo, and the Sugpiat or Pacific Yupik, who just like the Inuit or Inuuk, are different communities of Arctic Indians, that reside in wigwams and constantly fished and foraged, in the North Polar Region. From that large expanse in Canada to the United States, there are Native Americans such as the Havasupai, Zuni, Keres and Peeposh, who are Southwest Indians, which lived in tipis, hunted buffalos and bisons, carried the axe called the Tomhikon, along with other Native Americans, became the First Ecologists on the North American Continent. The numerous generations of Native Americans eventually became specialised communities of Arctic Indians, and other groupings, such as the Boreal Indians, and the Pacific Northwest Coast Indians. Some of them became communally distinct as the Northwest Plateau Indians, Great Plains Indians, Eastern Woodlands Indians, Great Basin Indians, California Indians and Southwest Indians. Over many thousands of years these American Indians held an intense alignment with the ecosystems and landscapes around them, because different geographic locations connect with the frequencies and vibrations which resonate beyond spacetime.

Every single Native American held an intense adoration for the Universal Creator and the Divine Creation. Hence, the ecosystems and landscapes of the North American Continent were revered as expressions of natural wonder. For example, the Abenaki used the word 'Tabaldak', to define the Universal Creator. The Narragansett used the word 'Cautantowwit', the Hopi Pueblo Indians used the word 'Taiowa', and the Snohomish used 'Dohkwibuhch'. Hence, the Native Americans have always believed that their own spiritual development is entirely resonant with the Universal Creator and the natural environments around them.

Many incredible Native American Star People Legends have been preserved as spiritually important stories, which reveal how much of American Indian Folklore is actually connected to the presence of Extraterrestrials on Planet Earth, in the Solar System and the rest of the Physical Universe. These kinds of stories emerged over many generations because the Native Americans, had been regularly contacted by Extraterrestrials, who then spiritually influenced the American Indians. Although this information can be difficult to accept, because it challenges the conventional thinking of the Western World, the various communities of American Indians have encountered the different kinds of Extraterrestrials who visit Planet Earth for thousands of years.

There are so many references in Native American Mythology to the Heavens, where they describe having interactions with certain kinds of Ultraterrestrials and Extraterrestrials that dwell in the starry reaches of the Milky Way Galaxy. Because of this, numerous American Indians believe there is a connection to the civilisations on the planets and moons that orbit the stellar mass called Taygeta, which is located in the Pleiades Star Cluster.

This grouping of stellar masses are located in the Taurus Constellation. Many of the stories from Greek Mythology mention that the Pleiades Star Cluster were actually known as the Eptá Aderfés (Seven Sisters) and M45 Star Cluster, which became an interstellar area that has a profound historical connection with Planet Earth. The different Native Americans, that have continually encountered the Ultraterrestrials and Extraterrestrials who originate from the Pleiades Star Cluster, define them as the Star People, which reside in the Shining Palaces of the Heavens.

Because so much of the history about the Native American Tribes, was deliberately censored and destroyed by White Europeans, whilst they colonised the New World of North America, it is difficult to find extensive amounts of information about the connections which existed between the Native Americans and the

Star People who reside on the planets and moons of Taygeta. Every story that has been told by the American Indians, concerning the Ultraterrestrials and Extraterrestrials who they observed departing from their Shining Palaces to visit the Planet Earth in their silverish discs. Hence, we can only focus on the stories and evidence which have been preserved.

The communities of Hopi Pueblo Indians use the word 'Anu,' which means 'Ant or 'Pincher', and the word 'Naki,' that means 'Friends', to describe the aliens known as the 'Anunaki', meaning 'Ant Friends' or 'Pincher Friends.' Apparently, these aliens were said to have come from planets and moons which orbit Zeta Reticuli A and Zeta Reticuli B, that are located in the Reticulum Constellation. Such unusual looking aliens may have been the Anunnaki, which the Sumerians, Akkadians, Babylonians and Assyrians, worshipped as Cosmic Deities. From the perspective of the Hopi Pueblo Indians, the aliens called the 'Anunaki', were the definable 'Ant Friends' or 'Pincher Friends', which many individuals know are the Zeta Reticulan Type A Grays and Zeta Reticulan Type B Grays, that are sometimes called the Short Grays.

Over thousands of years the Short Grays consistently visited the Fertile Crescent of the Arabian Peninsula. They were accompanied by some of the Aldebarians that are likewise known as the Nordic Giants, alongside some of the Orion Grays, and certain Draco Reptoids. Whilst the aliens explored the Fertile Crescent of the Arabian Peninsula, they established the civilisation of Sumeria, which existed where Iraq is located today. Many petroglyphs from the cities of Lagash, Umma, Larsa, Uruk, Nippur and Kish, in Sumeria, delineated the Short Grays, just as petroglyphs at Tutuveni, along the bottom of Echo Cliffs, in Northern Arizona, portrayed the Short Grays and other aliens.

The Hopi Pueblo Indians carved depictions of the Ant Friends or Pincher Friends, because they believed the aliens had travelled from planets and moons which orbit Zeta Reticuli A and B, that are located in the Reticulum Constellation. What message were the Hopi Pueblo Indians trying to convey by carving these petroglyphs? From what is known, it does appear that the Short Grays had some kind of interstellar connection with the Aldebarians, the Orion Grays, and the Draco Reptoids. Why have such aliens covertly worked together for so long?

For the Hopi Pueblo Indians and many other Native American Tribes, prayers were believed to be a method they could use to reach out to the Star People or the Star Brothers. Over thousands of years, the Hopi Pueblo Indians defined the spacecraft of the Star People, with the word 'Paatuwvota', which means 'Flying Shields' and every description of such glowing spacecraft confirms that each of them was an Unidentified Flying Object (UFO).

A very important story that symbolises the connections between the Native
Americans and the Extraterrestrials from planets and moons which orbit Taygeta, concerns the rock formation called Devils Tower, which is located in the Bear Lodge Mountains of the Western United States. We are told in the story which has been told by Craig Howe that the Devils Tower was called Mato Tipila (Bears Lodge) by the Lakota Indians, who are likewise known as the Teton Sioux.

According to the story there had once been Seven Maidens who had travelled across the Heavens, before landing next to Devils Tower National Monument. Once there, each of the Seven Maidens were chased by a bearlike Humanoid around the Devils Tower National Monument, and into the nearby countryside.

On their knees, the Seven Maidens prayed to the Heavens, and the ground beneath then erupted, lifting the Seven Maidens out of harm, as the bearlike Humanoid clawed at the risen ground and then carved vertical features into the Devils Tower National Monument. After this happened the Seven Maidens then returned into the Heavens, where they became radiantly placed in the Pleiades Star Cluster. Were the Seven Maidens interstellar travelling Extraterrestrials?

From what is mentioned in the stories of the Lakota Indians, who are likewise known as the Teton Sioux, the actual formation of Devils Tower National Monument began about 160,000 years ago when the Seven Maidens had descended to Planet Earth from the Star World of Taygeta, which is part of the Pleiades Star Cluster. Therefore, some kind of link obviously existed between the Pleiades Star Cluster and the Lakota Indians and other Native Americans, which as continued for many generations. What happened exactly at Devils Tower is open to debate, but there certainly was some kind of unusual event, which now seems to have been forgotten.

In the book called The Sacred Ways Of A Lakota, the authors known as Wallace Black Elk and William Sheldon Lyon, write about the renowned Wichasa Wakhan (Medicine Man) and Heyoka (Jester) of the Oglala Lakota Indians, who was called Hehaka Sapa and Black Elk. For many years Hehaka Sapa told stories about the interactions he had experienced with alien spacecraft, and on a certain occasion he stated:

"So When I Went To Vision Quest, That Disk Came From Above. The Scientists Call That A Unidentified Flying Object (UFO), But That's A Joke, See?"

The famous Lakotan Indian called Hehaka Sapa, who became commonly known as Black Elk, then mentioned that the *"Disk Landed"* above him and it *"Was Concave, And There Was Another One On Top Of That. It Was Silent, But It Lit And Luminesced Like Neon Lights. Even The Sacred Robes There Were Luminescent."*

Another interaction between a Native American and a spacecraft happened during the 13 October 1945. Because this event happened before the Roswell Incident, we need to consider that these kinds of Extraterrestrials have been visiting American Indians for thousands of years before North America was colonised.

During the 15 August 1932, a designated Geologist, Robert Hallum, from the United States Bureau of Mines (USBM), which is part of the U.S. Interior Department, accompanied by a Geophysicist, Edward Thompson, from the United States Geological Survey (USGS), had both gone to the Jornada Bat Caves on the Armendaris Ranch, to carry out a mineral study and inspection. They had travelled from the nearby the city of Truth Or Consequences, in Sierra County. Like many other locations in South Western New Mexico, the Armendaris Ranch had become a place where supernatural activity had become the normality. After entering the opening both Robert Hallum and Edward Thompson then discovered a triangle shaped metallic spacecraft, and the bodies of what appeared to be Zeta Reticulan Type A Grays and Zeta Reticulan Type B Grays. After they encountered the spacecraft and bodies of the aliens, they left the Jornada Bat Caves and eventually mentioned to colleagues what had transpired.

On the 7 June 1934, a speleologist called Gerald Mitchell, found an identical metallic spacecraft and a body of a Short Gray in the Carlsbad Caverns of the Chihuahuan Desert. Many kinds of UFO sightings had been seen over the Carlsbad Caverns before the spacecraft and body of the Short Gray were found by Gerald Mitchell. Additionally, sightings of alien spacecraft has been seen over the nearby city of Carlsbad, which is situated in Eddy County. Just like with the village of Loving in South Eastern New Mexico, the city of Carlsbad has always been a place where alien spacecraft have been present.

The story about how the 12 year old Dakota Indian called Mahpiya Wambli and his grandfather encountered a contingent of Extraterrestrials, is truly incredible. During the evening of the 13 October 1945, Mahpiya Wambli and his grandfather were resting at their home on the Yankton Indian Reservation, in South Dakota. Suddenly they heard a tremendous crashing noise which made the horses flee across the surrounding meadows. The grandfather went out to fetch the horses the next day.
Whilst he was doing this, the grandfather of Mahpiya Wambli discovered some kind of newly formed crater in the middle of a nearby meadow. So the grandfather spoke with Mahpiya about what he had seen, and they both decided to walk back out to the newly formed crater. After they got to the crater both Mahpiya and his grandfather noticed that in the bottom of the crater was

some kind of metallic spacecraft. What appeared to be an unusual luminescence could be seen coming from an open doorway. Both of them decided to take a look.

Once they had briefly had a look around, both Mahpiya Wambli and his grandfather found some Extraterrestrials in a navigation room, that were about 8 feet tall. Apparently, the contingent of Extraterrestrials wore shimmering green suits, and each of them had seemingly hairless translucent complexions and eyes which changed colour.

The surprised Extraterrestrials were shocked by the appearance of Mahpiya Wambli and his grandfather. As soon as the grandfather spoke to them, the gathered Extraterrestrials immediately disappeared. Mahpiya and his grandfather did not feel any fear whilst they observed the aliens, because the cultures of the Native Americans have long believed that Extraterrestrials are the Star People who have a shared genetic heritage with Humans.

After this encounter, they returned to their house. Over the next four weeks, the Star People which both of them had seen, were observed walking around the property. The contingent of Extraterrestrials appeared to be gathering rocks, plants and lichens as samples they could study. After a few days, the aliens started to like Mahpiya and his grandfather, and therefore invited them onto their interstellar spacecraft.

Once Mahpiya and his grandfather were inside the spacecraft, the highly psychic Extraterrestrials then communicated with both Mahpiya and his grandfather by using telepathy. According to the Extraterrestrials, they were forced to live below ground in domed Crystal

Cities, on planets and moons that are far beyond this Solar System. The reason for this was because the landmasses of their planets and moons had become so dry and arid. The aliens then explained that each of them had been covertly visiting Planet Earth for over 15,000 years but had rarely interacted with Humans during that time. I wonder why the aliens hardly ever communicated with Humans?

There is more to this story, because after the Extraterrestrials left the Planet Earth behind and went home to the Heavens, they did not return. Soon after the incident had occurred a contingent of Security Police from the U.S. Air Force, stationed at Ellsworth Air Force Base, in Pennington County, then cordoned off the area on the Yankton Indian Reservation. Many bizarre UFO sightings had been observed there and elsewhere in Western South Dakota. Because the Security Police from the U.S. Air Force had been monitoring the UFO activity over the Yankton Indian Reservation, they knew about the alien spacecraft. Hence, the Security Police confiscated the property and meadows owned by the grandfather of Mahpiya. The U.S. Air Force then filled the crater with water, to conceal the facts about the landing of the alien spacecraft. Even though this seems to be a fictional story, the events which have been described appear to have arisen from a very unusual interaction that really did happen.

Another Native American Tribe, called the Ashiwi Indians or Zuni Pueblo Indians, talk of the Star People, which they believe were their genetic ancestors who had travelled from beyond our Solar System. The communities of Ashiwi Indians or Zuni Pueblo Indians, have always stated that whenever the Extraterrestrials visited Planet Earth, they would bring new supernal knowledge and give support to themselves and other Native Americans.

One of the Elders known as Clifford Mahooty, like certain other Zuni Indians, was a Kachina Society Priest, who used to inform his relatives and friends about how the grandfathers told him that a spiritual connection had once existed between the Ashiwi Indians or Zuni Pueblo Indians, and the Star People or the Space Brothers, for thousands of years.

Clifford Mahooty also explained that the communication methods of the Ashiwi Elders or Zuni Pueblo Elders, had been originally conveyed with telepathic symbols and glyphs, by the Star People or the Space Brothers. Some of these aliens continue to visit and interact with the Native Americans in different remote locations along the Little Colorado River in Western New Mexico. Over the last 25 years this kind of communication has become concisely defined as the Hyperspace Language.

Many fascinating stories have been told about the Star People who have spent years communicating with the Native Americans because they have a spiritual connection with the visiting Ultraterrestrials and Extraterrestrials who collectively exist beyond spacetime. There were large communities of American Indian Tribes who inhabited the vast wilderness. However, the Arctic Indians, as with other Native Americans, such as the Boreal Indians and the Pacific Northwest Coast Indians, have been largely erased, suppressed and censored because the Elites and their Secret Societies found it so difficult to control their spirituality. Over many generations, the same happened to the Northwest Plateau Indians, Great Plains Indians, Eastern Woodlands Indians, Great Basin Indians,

California Indians and Southwest Indians. Even though aspects of the worship which the Native Americans once used to exemplify Mother Nature have physically gone, the essence of their beliefs remains within the ecosystems and landscapes of North America, and no one should underestimate the potency of their knowledge. We must remember how important developing a spiritual awareness is, because the parameters which define the 3D Holographic Reality of this Material Dimension have been partially inverted, to consistently limit the self.

CHAPTER 5: THE CIVILISATION OF TARTARIA

Because of the numerous maps and other kinds of historical evidence which clearly show the civilisation of Tartaria did exist in Northern Russia, when the towns and cities of Tartaria disappeared from history, a cultural inversion seemingly emerged. The civilisation of Tartaria was spiritually and technologically very advanced. Every one of the Tartarians existed with tremendous abundance. Indeed, the landmass of Great Tartaria was known as the Golden Empire, and extended across Siberia which is also defined as Northern Asia. Originally the landmass of Tartaria had been ruled by the Tatarskiye Velikany (Mighty Giants), who were essentially Aryans. Tartaria would have still been the largest ruled geographic area today, if the Mud Floods or some other comparable set of upheavals had not destroyed everything there.

During the 4 October 1586 the civilisation of Tartaria, which means 'Strong Place,' was established, but over many centuries the spiritual unity of that geographic expanse then began to fragment. After the 30 December 1922 Tartaria was separated into administrative territories, and one of these became the Tatarstan Republic, which is also called the Tataria Republic, that is part of the Russian Federation. Once upon a time the landmass of Tartaria extended across the vastness of Northern Asia, where the civilisation extended to the borders of Siberia, and was called Great Tartary.

On the 18 April 1627, the famous Dutch Cartographer known as Willem Janszoon Blaeu, completed his map of Tartaria, which clearly showed how massive the expanse of the Tartarian Civilisation actually was. The map showed Tartaria reached the borders of China and

Mongolia. This incredible advanced culture used free energy systems, grandiose architecture that still exist to this day, using the electromagnetic frequencies of Planet Earth to abundantly live in Tartaria.

On the 15 January 2013, the President Vladimir Vladimirovich Putin, inaugurated a new archive with the Russian Geographical Society and Russian Academy of Sciences, where maps of Tartaria have been made widely available to the Russian People. This gesture gave Planet Earth a clearance that the Russian Federation is embarking on a cultural process of revealing its true history, because Vladimir Putin is aware that a country that does not know its history cannot have an effective and cohesive spiritual future.

During the 1 February 2017, Vladimir Vladimirovich Putin and Dmitry Anatolyevich Medvedev, met with the former President of Tatarstan, who had become the State Councillor of the Republic of Tatarstan, Mintimer Sharipovich Shaimiev, to present him with a map of Tartarus. The map had been made by the famous Dutch Cartographer Willem Janszoon Blaeu. So how did Willem Blaeu know how to draw and outline the contours of Tartaria if the landmass never existed?

On the gold-framed map the territory of North Eastern Eurasia, from the Volga and the Caspian Sea, and from westward reaches to the Eastern Ocean, belonged to the civilisation of Tartaria. Even though we learn about Dynastic Egypt, Classical Greece, and the Persian Empire, the Ottoman Turks, and the Romans, in schools, colleges and universities, all of this history is only a partial glimpse into the past. Much of what really occurred has been censored and deleted when it comes to academics looking at the missing historical aspects that concern the Tartarian Empire. Although most of the conventional scholars refuse to accept the notion that perhaps the Tartarian Empire really did exist, and was more advanced than the Western World, there is large amounts of evidence to prove the civilisation of Tartaria did exist in Northern Asia.

The landmass and territory called Tartary and Great Tartary was an historical location in Northern Asia, that existed between the Caspian Sea, the Ural Mountains, and the Pacific Ocean. From the perspective of Western Europeans, the landmass of Tartary was a blanket term that was used to define many of areas in Central Asia, Northern Asia, and Eastern Asia. Because these geographic locations were largely unknown to explorers from the United Kingdom and Mainland Europe, it became easier for them to define such locations as parts of Tartaria.

Hence, the entire geographic territory became commonly known as Tartary, and the inhabitants were called the Tartars. After the 31 August 1742, an understanding of the geography increased as explorers named the landmass. Many of the academics from Mainland Europe began to subdivide Tartary into territorial sections with prefixes that denoted the name of the local ruler or the specific geographical location. Thus, Siberia became Great Tartary or Russian Tartary, the Crimean Khanate became Little Tartary, the area of North Eastern China which had become defined as Manchuria, then became Chinese Tartary, and Western Central Asia became known as Independent Tartary.

During the 22 July 1998, the CIA declassified a document called '*National Cultural Development Under Communism*,' which they had produced on the 1 June

1957. A section within the document mentions the existence of the Tartar Civilisation, and how its once incredible presence had to be censored and deleted. Here is a quote from the document that summarises how any knowledge about Tartaria had to be kept from the public.

"In Other Words, Tarter History Was To Be Rewritten, Let Us Be Frank, Was To Be Falsified, In Order To Eliminate References To The Great Russian Aggressions And To Hide Facts Of The Real Centre Of Tarter-Russian Relations."

James William Lee wrote a book called '*The One World Tartarians: The Greatest Civilisation Ever To Be Erased From History*', where he explains how the historical presence of Tartaria was deliberately censored and deleted. According to the book, numerous remnant buildings were left intact after the Mud Floods destroyed the civilisation of Tartaria, and yet the landmass and its communities have seemingly been completely forgotten.

The word 'Tartaria' is linguistically connected with the Greek word 'Tartaros', which means Frightful Place. That subterranean location then became more commonly known as Tartarus. In the stories of Greek Mythology, the anciently founded Cyclopean Giants were put into gloomy depths of Tartaros (Frightful Place). Hence, the Cyclopean Giants of Greek Mythology represented the Tartarian Giants, whose Golden Empire was submerged beneath vast amounts of silt and soil during the Mud Floods. The collective psychological trauma which arose from the devastation of the Tartarian Civilisation was remembered in these archetypal stories. According to what is known, it appears that the elusive Mighty Giants would grow to 8 feet to 12 feet in height, and therefore, as the Cyclopean Giants from Greek Mythology, were of massive stature, this was also used to represent the huge physiques of the inhabitants that once existed across Northern Asia.

The communities of Tatarskiye Velikany (Mighty Giants), are thought to have been Breatharians, which meant they did not have to rely on the consumption of food and water for calories. Such massive Humanoids therefore did not use digestion to absorb the vitamins and minerals their bodies required. Instead, the resourceful Mighty Giants, received sustenance directly from the aether and the geomagnetic frequencies which resonate around the Planet Earth. This meant the Mighty Giants, had obtained a true mastery as Breatharians, as the aether is comprised of electrostatic frequencies and vibrations in the troposphere, stratosphere and ionosphere of Planet Earth. Since the Tartarian Giants were Breatharians, it is possible they had digestive systems that were very different to those of Human Beings.

Over many generations the highly efficient civilisation of Tartarian became known as the Tatarskoye Tsarstvo (Mighty Empire), which extended across Northern Asia, before then developing across the Northern Hemisphere. Eventually the Tartarian Giants travelled into the North American Continent. Great Tartaria was the largest controlled geographic expanse, and would have still been the largest to this day, if the Mud Floods had not occurred. The extensive Golden Empire of Tartaria, flourished partly because the civilization knew how to effectively use and integrate Occult Technology and telluric electricity with the grandiose architecture of the buildings which the Mightly Giants had constructed over many generations.

The iron and steel decorative roof ridge crestings of the buildings in Tartaria functioned as fractal antennae, which consistently absorbed the flowing telluric currents of the atmosphere and geomagnetic leylines, which the Tartarian Giants ensured were installed on every building.

Apparently the communities of Tartarian Giants had free energy systems installed within their churches, temples and every other kind of building. Hence, every property functioned as some kind of aetheric generator facility, that produced electricity from the geomagnetic frequencies which resonate around the Planet Earth. Maybe there is a connection to the scientific research of the Serbian inventor, Nikola Tesla. How was he able to initiate the development of his incredible experiments? The communities of Mighty Giants also used other buildings such as water towers functioned as resonant acoustic healing center in Tartaria, because the Mighty Giants knew how to harness the telluric electrical currents of Planet Earth.

By using ingenious engineering, intricate architectural features, and Occult Technology, the immensely productive Mighty Giants transformed the electrostatic soil into a natural telluric circuit of the ground. Hence, the civilisation of Tartaria exemplified a sense of abundance by using such geomagnetic energies, as they consistently resonate around Planet Earth.

The communities of Tartarian Giants had advanced technological methods of capturing and storing the ever present telluric energies, by using electrical capacitors that could heat and ventilate their own buildings. The fireplaces which the Tartarians constructed inside their buildings did not actually burn any combustible substances like they do today. Instead, the fireplaces of the Tartarian Giants were used as a electrical heating and cooling source for the houses and other buildings of the Tartarians. Hence, these incredible Humanoids were able to connect with the telluric currents of Planet Earth, so they could store and use the boundless electricity. So where has this information gone? Why does nobody ever talk about the civilisation of Tartaria?

Further evidence points to the fact that the Tartarian Civilisation was eradicated by a number of Mud Floods which occurred between 1740 and 1894. Such upheavals became known as the Great Reset, and were used by the Secret Societies to further their own plans and objectives.

The First Mud Flood occurred after The Great Frost, which began during the 8 January 1740, and ended on the 6 October 1741. Apparently the sudden climate change in the Northern Hemisphere was caused by a massive eruption of the Sheveluch Volcano in North Eastern Russia. Vast atmospheric disturbances happened and possibly led to the Second Mud Flood which became widespread on the 29 October 1834, which then brought about the Great Reset of the 12 February 1835. During these specific years, the Little Ice Age which had lasted from the 17 December 1650 to the 15 April 1832, therefore became a long term atmospheric process which included the weather conditions that were defined as The Great Frost. However, once the climate began to get warmer, the overall thawing resulted in massive riverine and fluvial changes, which led to the Second Mud Flood becoming an extensive disaster.

Subsequent volcanic eruptions occurred, and these upheavals also caused atmospheric changes. Such events might have become factors which contributed towards the Third Mud Flood, which happened on the 7 June 1892. The Third Mud Flood largely destroyed the remnants of Great Tartaria, and then by the 30 April 1894, everything had geographically changed on Planet Earth.

There are thousands of buildings on Planet Earth that are over 250 years old, which are encased in a silt, gravel and soil from this Mud Floods, and therefore indicate that such events actually did occur. Much of the silt, gravel and soil covers many stories of the remnant buildings, and in some cases has even completely engulfed them. This was most definitely an older kind of Great Reset, and was exploited and used as the perfect opportunity to eradicate the advanced scientific knowledge which Humans could have used. We have to remember that knowledge is power.

Over the past 5,000 years there have been several Great Resets of civilisations, from the time of the Thúr Bháibil (Confusion Tower), that is mentioned within Irish Folklore, and because of the subsequent Mud Floods. However, the most recent Great Reset was also the result of the Mud Floods, and therefore explains why there are so many anomalous features in the architectural designs of various buildings which have been observed in many countries.

When we look at North America and elsewhere on Planet Earth, its suggests that there were advanced civilisations which existed from around 1627 to 1835, and in many cases, even earlier than that. We are told American Indians resided in teepees or wikiups, but this is a very distorted version of history, when actually only a minority of Native Americans existed like that. The communities of American Indians developed highly advanced spiritual cultures, but much of that true history has also been completely destroyed.

So did the civilisation of Tartaria exist? The idea that a Golden Empire historically existed in Northern Asia sounds like a story from a Hollywood movie. But there is no doubt that Tartaria was real because of the evidence which has been discovered. So why is this information not taught in schools, colleges and universities? Why is so much information about Tartaria deliberately kept from the public? The German Philosopher and Economist called Karl Heinrich Marx stated in one sentence how the Elites have always tried to manipulate the perceptions of Humans, when he said *"Keep People From Their History, And They Are Easily Controlled."*

The controlling structures of the Elites and their Secret Societies, have been designed to conceal the real history of Planet Earth, because anything that does fit the narrative which they use immediately contradicts the 3D Holographic Reality of this Material Dimension, which they want you to identify with. Hence, the Elites have to keep censoring and deleting the various prehistoric truths. But they can never erase the concealed knowledge about Tartaria, because evidence will always continue to arise. It is our responsibility to solve this incredible puzzle and learn from this spiritual experience as Human Beings, as we need to remember how important the truth history of Planet Earth has become.

CHAPTER 6: PRIMORDIAL GIANTS

Did a civilisation of Giants once exist on Planet Earth? But once you begin to explore this subject it becomes clear that a lot of the history classes which are taught in schools, colleges and universities are used to convey information that is largely incorrect and does not make any sense. This is partly because much of the truth which concerns the prehistoric times has been deliberately edited and deleted, to conceal the fact that thousands of years ago communities of Giants did rule vast geographic expanses on Planet Earth. We must remember that in the Old Testament of the Holy Bible, it mentions the following information about the Primordial Giants.

"There Were Giants In The Earth In Those Days; And Also After That, When The Sons Of God Came In Unto The Daughters Of Men, And They Bare Children To Them, The Same Became Mighty Men Which Were Of Old, Men Of Renown." - Genesis 6:4

The current perception of a Giant is a big looking Humanoid who is defined as 7 feet tall and more. However, hundreds of skeletons have been found on Planet Earth which easily reach 10 feet and more in height. Across the expanses of North America and Central America, massive skeletons have been founded by archaeologists who are employed by the Smithsonian Institution in Washington DC, and many of the skeletons were 12 feet to 16 feet high.

Many of the Archeology Curators and Museum Curators at the Smithsonian Institution, in New York City (NYC) on Long Island, have covertly been involved with the retrieval of enormous skeletons that had come from coastlines of Santa Catalina Island, which is in Southern California. Other employees of the Smithsonian Institution who carry out research in the city of Cambridge in Northern Massachusetts, have also examined the skeletons of Giants, just as they have in the Census Designated Place (CDP) of Chantilly in North Eastern Virginia. Some of the massive skeletons that have been found in Mexico, Guatemala, Columbia and Ecuador were transported to facilities which are managed by the Smithsonian Tropical Research Institute (STRI) within Panama City and the location of Amador, in the Panamá Oeste Province of Central Panama.

The individual known Robert Pershing Wadlow is the tallest Human to have existed in recorded history on Planet Earth. He was a Giant that stood 8 feet 11 inches. However, both of his parents were normal sized. His immense stature and his continued growth in adulthood were due to hypertrophy of the pituitary gland, which results in abnormal levels of growth hormones becoming very prevalent in Humans. Does the medical condition known as hypertrophy have any kind of genetic and biological connection with the Giants who used to exist on Planet Earth? Did prehistoric gravitational differences have anything to do with the size of the Primordial Giants that once ruled in Britain, Mainland Europe and North America?
Certain parts of Hindu Folklore mention the Dānavaḥ (River Giants), who used to inhabit the tributary of the Ganges River, called the Yamuna River, which flows through the city of Delhi and elsewhere in in North Eastern India. Apparently, these kinds of Indian Giants had descended the Vedic Sage called Kashyapa Upadhyay and the Hindu Goddess, Danu Prajapatni, who was a Tārakīya Īśvara (Astral Deity).

The photographer and traveller known as Professor James Ricalton, attended the mass celebratory gathering called the Delhi Durbar on the 1st January 1903 at the National Capital Territory of Delhi. Professor James Ricalton had travelled around Planet Earth and during the Delhi Durbar, he posed with the Kashmir Giants, who were also called the Cashmere Giants, before having photographs taken of them. Both these individuals that Professor James Ricalton photographed were twin brothers, called Harbhajan Dhariwal and Barindra Dhariwal. They were employed as Royal Guardsmen for Maharaja Amar Singh at the Amar Mahal Palace in the city of Jammu. Apparently, Maharaja Amar Singh also owned luscious farmland near to his residency in the Princely State of Kashmir and Jammu, in Northern India. The first Kashmir Giant, known as Harbhajan Dhariwal, was 7 feet 4 inches tall and the other, Barindra Dhariwal, was 7 feet 9 inches tall.

Various legends of the Native Ecuadorians such as the Caranqui, Otavaleños, Cayambi, and the Pichincha, have stories which recount a prehistoric time when massive Giants who stood 28 feet tall. Additionally, the Chimbuelo, Panzaleo, Salasacan, and Tungurahua, have encountered the same Giants, which apparently inhabit the Ecuadorian Jungle and the Cordillera Occidental Range of the Andean Mountains. Other communities of Native Ecuadorians which include the Waranka, Tugua, Puruhá, Cañari, and the Saraguro, have also observed the Giants over many aeons. Wherever the Primordial Giants from the Atlantean Continent walked on Planet Earth, they would construct huge megalithic urban dwellings, and it seems to be the case that the Ecuadorian Giants were possibly connected with the civilisation of Atlantis.

During the 18 April 1965 remains of a massive skeleton were found by a Catholic Priest called Father Carlos Miguel Vaca Alvarado, in the Changaiminas (Deities Cemetery) of the Ecuadorian Jungle. From what Father Carlos Miguel Vaca Alvarado had found, it appears that the skeleton of a Ecuadorian Giant was over 10,000 years old. They estimated the size of the Ecuadorian Giant was said to be around 25 feet tall. Because other fragments of skeletons that were found, the Catholic Priest believed that other Gigantes Ecuatorianos (Ecuadorian Giants) must have perished there as well. Apparently the Ecuadorian Giants who had inhabited the urban area that has been described as the Ciudad Perdida (Lost City), were around 27 feet tall. Many residents from Gonzanamá believe that communities of Ecuadorian Giants once existed where their small village is located in the Loja Province of Southern Ecuador.

The explorers known as Manuel Chauvin, Bolivar Morales, Luis Fernando Villacreses, Manuel Viera and Jhon Vinueza, were involved with the discovery of the pyramidal structure in the Amazon Jungle of Central Ecuador. According to what has been mentioned, the Poder Ejecutivo (Executive Branch) of the Gobierno Ecuatoriano (Ecuadorian Government) with President Rafael Vicente Correa Delgado, made the necessary technical and logistical arrangements so this area of the Amazon Jungle could be properly examined after the archaeological discoveries had been made on the 16 March 2012. Once the pyramidal structure had been inspected, the explorers known as Manuel Chauvin, Bolivar Morales, Luis Fernando Villacreses, Manuel Viera and Jhon Vinueza, ascertained that the structure was at least 12,000 year old. Although nobody can actually confirm who actually built the pyramidal structures, the fact that skeletons of Ecuadorian Giants have been found in many geographic locations across the Pacific Coastal Region of Western Ecuador, the Andes Region of Central Ecuador and the Amazon Region of Eastern Ecuador, indicates that such findings do have some kind of connection to the unusual prehistoric buildings which have been found everywhere.

The author and researcher Bruce Fenton reported during the 15 March 2012 to the 16 March 2012 a contingent of explorers and scientists discovered a pyramidal structure in the Amazon Jungle of Central Ecuador, that was constructed from igneous and metamorphic crystalline basement rocks, which were mainly comprised of granite. The archaeological discovery was made by Manuel Chauvin, Bolivar Morales, Luis Fernando Villacreses, Manuel Viera and Jhon Vinueza. They were helped by volunteers such as Ricardo Jimenez, Alvarez Hidalgo, Fernando Gomez and Miguel Pacheco. Because of the unusual artifacts, relics and massive skeletons that were found, Manuel Chauvin, Bolivar Morales, Luis Fernando Villacreses, Manuel Viera and Jhon Vinueza, defined the location as the Lost City of the Ecuadorian Giants. Many artifacts, relics and massive skeletons were found by them, with the help of Ricardo Jimenez, Alvarez Hidalgo, Fernando Gomez and Miguel Pacheco. Different kinds of hugely oversized tools were found that could have only been used by the Ecuadorian Giants. Numerous holes had been drilled through the centre of granite rocks. The discovery of the Lost City of the Ecuadorian Giants is one of the most important archaeological discoveries that has ever been made on Planet Earth.

During the 5 October 1936, the French Archaeologists known as Jean Paul Lebeuf and Marcel Griaule, led an excursion to Chad, in North Central Africa. Whilst they crossed the landmass Jean Paul Lebeuf and Marcel Griaule observed some areas covered with small mounds. They decided to excavate the mounds and found the remains of 10 feet skeletons of Humanoids who were called the Saos Giants.

The country of Chad is a remote landmass that is controlled by the petrochemical industries that have their origins in countries such as the United Kingdom, the French Republic, the Peoples Republic of China, and the United States of America. Because of the ethnic intricacies of Chad, it is known as The Babel Tower of Planet Earth. Both gold and uranium mining industries are widespread there. Even though ecosystems have been destroyed in that part of Africa, concealed prehistoric knowledge has been preserved in the landmass. But just like with the Indian Tribes of the North American Continent, the internecine Elites and their Secret Societies have ensured that most truths about the actual history of Planet Earth must remain concealed from Humans.

On the 10 August 1891, the New York Times reported that during the 7 August 1891 designated Archeology Curators and Museum Curators from the Smithsonian Institution had discovered several large "*Pyramidal Monuments*" at Lake Mills, near the city of Madison, in Southern Wisconsin. "*Madison Was In Ancient Days The Center Of A Teeming Population Numbering Not Less Than 200,000,*" the New York Times said. The excavators which the Archeology Curators and Museum Curators from the Smithsonian Institution had used, found an elaborate pattern of defensive works which they believed the White Giants had constructed, and named the fortified structure Fort Aztalan. During the 20 December 1897, the New York Times followed up with a report on three large burial mounds that had been discovered in the town of Maple Creek, in Outagamie County, on the 16 December 1897. According to the Menomini Indians, Ojibwe Indians, Potawatomi Indians and Hoocagra Indians, this area of North Eastern Wisconsin had once been the ruled over by the White Giants.

Across the North American Continent, the communities of Native Americans have customs which go back over 60,000 years, and during this expanse of time, many of the American Indians would have experienced countless interactions with the White Giants and the Hairy Giants. For example, we have the 18 skeletons of the Wisconsin Giants that were discovered by academics from Beloit College at Lake Lawn Farm, which is near to Lake Delavan, in Walworth County, on the 26 April 1912. This case was reported on the 4 May 1912 issue of the New York Times. Just like with many other areas of Southern Wisconsin, the location where the Wisconsin Giants were found has always been known to be very supernatural. The obviously related kinds of Wisconsin Giants were found to have stood 9 feet 4 inches to 10 feet 8 inches in height.

The customs of the Choctaw Indians, always mentioned that Nahullo (White Giants) once inhabited Tennessee State. Over many generations there had been continual battles which had arisen between the Choctaw Indians and the aggressive Nahullo (White Giants). According to the stories of the Choctaw Indians, the communities of Nahullo (White Giants) were at least 10 feet high, and they would reside by the vast subterranean rivers which ran beneath where the South Eastern Woodlands used to be located. However, that area became known as Alabama and Mississippi, in the South Eastern United States. Many of the Nahullo (White Giants) were also known to be experts at navigating the riverways that led into the Hollow Earth.

Seemingly there were Irish Celtic Aryans, who once resided in small villages in Louisiana, Mississippi, Alabama, Florida, Tennessee, Kentucky, Arkansas, North Carolina, South Carolina and Georgia. Each of these locations are situated in the South Eastern United States. Hence, it appears as if the Irish Celtic Tribes established settlements in North America before the arrival of Christopher Columbus. According to the Dawhee Indians, the communities of Duhare Giants from South Carolina, were originally from Ireland. The various Duhare Giants were described as standing over 7 feet tall, and had greyish blue eyes, very tanned olive complexions, red to pale brown hair and massive physiques.

The communities of Northern Paiute Indians from North Eastern California, have always remembered the reddish haired Giants which they spent thousands of years fighting with. Over many generations, the resourceful Northern Paiute Indians became used to encountering the Giants within parts of North Western Nevada, Eastern Oregon, and Southern Idaho. Further to such events, is the fact that many of the Southern Paiute Indians from Northern Arizona, South Western Utah, and Southern Nevada, also had encounters with the same lifeforms.

The Lenni Lenape of Pennsylvania, in the North Eastern United States, talk of large White Giants that once excavated around the Appalachian Mountains and the Great Lakes Basin of the North Western United States and Central Canada. Many of the Lenni Lenape Indians have stories about how the White Giants had red and blonde hair. Are the Elites and their Secret Societies deliberately concealing the prehistoric truth about the fact that Giants use to exist on Planet Earth? Therefore, has this knowledge been deliberately suppressed to prevent Human Consciousness from spiritually developing?

There are a lot of references in the Holy Bible about the Gadolim (Giants), that were lifeforms which also became known as the Nephilim (Fallen Beings). Such creatures were the progenies of defiant Angels which decided to procreate with female Humans in the days before the Great Flood destroyed the civilisations of the Primordial Giants. Was the Great Flood in the Holy Bible deliberately created to eradicate the Primordial Giants from Planet Earth? Did some of them manage to retreat into the Hollow Earth?

The story of Dawid Ben Yishai and Golyat Ben Anak, better known David and Goliath, may be true or not, maybe a metaphorical story, but the Israelite known as David was still fighting the Philistine Giant of Canaan, who apparently stood nearly 10 feet tall. There are many stories in Greek Mythology which mention the Gígantes, Γίγαντες (Giants), who are likewise spoken of as the Titans, and whom are connected with the Cyclopses. The prehistoric Titans were known to fight the Olympian Deities and most Greek Mythology evolved from the consistent discord and strife.

Much of Norse Mythology is about the Hrímþursar (Frost Giants) and the Bálþursar (Fire Giants), that were massive lifeforms, which also known as the Eldrþursar (Fire Giants). Because of their etheric appearances, the huge Giants became further defined as the Logiþursar (Fire Giants) and the Hyrrþursar (Fire Giants). Such lifeforms had been supernaturally empowered by the Norse Deities. Generally, the Norse Deities represent benevolence while the Jötnar (Eaters) or the Jǫtnar (Eaters), are associated with malevolence. These enormous Giants were often perceived to be the ones who instigated conflicts with the Norse Deities, because they would take captured victims to the Jötunheim (Eaters Realm).

Both the Frost Giants and the Fire Giants played an essential role in the upheaval which became defined as Ragnarök (Doom For The Deities), and was also called Ragnarøkkr (Twilight For The Deities). This event represented the widespread electromagnetic destruction of the Physical Universe and therefore everything within it. Hence, the enormous upheavals of Ragnarök or Ragnarøkkr would also cleanse the Planet Earth, and bring about a spiritual resurgence.

There is the famous English Fairy Tale called Jack And The Beanstalk, where the Pagan Giant says *"Fee Fi Fo Fum, I Smell The Blood Of An Englishmen."* Is this not suggestive of the Primordial Giants intense hatred towards Humans? The story from English Folklore, called Jack And The Beanstalk, appears in *'The Story Of Jack Spriggins And The Enchanted Bean'* and *'The History of Jack And The Bean Stalk,' 'The Home Treasury'* and in English Fairy Tales. Additionally, the story called *'Jack The Giant Killer'* is about the conflict between the British Giants and the Celtic Britons, during the reign of King Arthur Pendragon. Much of Cornish Folklore in South West England, concerns the subject of

Giants, as does Breton Mythology and Welsh Bardic Folklore and some aspects of Norse Mythology.

We need to consider the notion that many of the prehistoric worship locations in the United Kingdom were quite possibly constructed by the British Giants. This means that locations such as Stonehenge, on Salisbury Plain, might have been created by the British Giants. Elsewhere in South East Wiltshire, are the remnants of worship locations that were probably constructed by the British Giants, or were imitated by the Druidic Priests. Many other locations in the United Kingdom were possible constructed by the British Giants, and these include the Avebury Circle in North Central Wiltshire, and the Rollright Stones in the Cotswolds of North West Oxfordshire.

There are stories from Scottish Folklore which describe how communities of Fuamhairean Boglach (Marsh Giants) use to reside on the Northern Isles of North East Scotland, where they constructed the Brodgar Ring or Brogar Ring, on the Orkney Island called Mainland, which is also known as Hrossey and Pomona. Along with this location, Castlerigg Stone Circle or the Keswick Carles, in the Lake District, was believed to have been assembled by the Fathaigh Ailbíonach (White Giants) who were also called the Fathaigh Goidiúil (Strange Giants). This location and the civil town of Keswick, in North West Cumbria are famous because of the ley lines which resonate in both of these areas. The Meini Hirion or Druids Circle in the town of Penmaenmawr is another location where a race of Cewri Cymreig (United Border Giants) or Cewri Brython (Painted Giants) were supposed to have founded their worshipful practices. Indeed, much of Conwy County Borough in North Wales has similar correlations with the Welsh Giants. Was there some kind of connection between the leylines of Celtic Britain and the British Giants?

Whilst the Roman Legions marched across Celtic Britain, any communities of Giants would have been looked upon as monstrous creatures, and would have been hated and feared. Just as the British Giants were seen as outcasts by the Celtic Britons, so were they by the Roman Legions. There are many stories from Italian Folklore of the Roman Legions who captured the Montem Gigantes (Mountain Giants) and Silvem Gigantes (Forest Giants), that were then sent to Rome. Although no evidence has ever become apparent, which could effectively confirm whether or not the British Giants actually existed, they became very well documented in Celtic Folklore. Maybe the only such lifeforms could be safe was to retreat into the Hollow Earth. Were there once Humanoids who had extremely large statures?

Was it any accident that when the Vietnam War began on the 1 November 1955, the area called the Plain of Jars or the Thong Hai Hin, became an important location for the General Officers and Senior Officers from the North Vietnamese Army (NVA) to visit. Across this area in the Xiangkhoang Plateau of Central Laos, as with elsewhere in South Eastern Asia, the legends of Primordial Giants have always been known about. Much of Laos Folklore mentions how the 24 feet to 28 feet tall Bung Nyakhainy (Marsh Giants) and the Pamai Nyakhainy (Forest Giants) once ruled that landmass, as they did across most of South Eastern Asia. The huge Giants were ruled by a Savan Kasad (Divine King), named Khun Cheung, who fought a long and ultimately victorious battle against the Laotians or Laos Tribes.

Even though no official announcement has ever been made in academic publications that include Scientific American, Science News, New Scientist, Popular Science, Cosmos Magazine, and National Geographic, concerning whether or not Giants existed on Planet Earth, it is certainly important to explore this fascinating subject and to consider the possible truths about the concealed past. Because the existence of Giants has never been confirmed, why has so much effort been made to suppress any knowledge about them if they were never real to begin with?

CHAPTER 7: HOLLOW EARTH ANOMALIES

The concept which has become defined as the Hollow Earth Theory (HET) can actually help you gain a completely different spiritual perspective. Even though the idea of a Hollow Earth is just a concept, numerous scientists and politicians consider the Hollow Earth Theory to be of tremendous importance. Many explorers have brought back stories from the observations they have made, whilst such individuals travel across the remotest areas of Planet Earth.

During the 10 April 1818, the individual known as John Cleves Symmes Junior, who was a Captain of the U.S. Army, published Circular Number 1 and distributed the document to colleges, politicians and various academics on Planet Earth.

"I Declare That The Earth Is Hollow And Habitable Within; Containing A Number Of Solid Concentric Spheres, One Within The Other, And That It Is Open At The Poles Twelve Or Sixteen Degrees. I Pledge My Life In Support Of This Truth, And Am Ready To Explore The Hollow, If The World Will Support And Aid Me In The Undertaking."

The truth is we know more about the surface of the Moon than we do about what lyes on the deepest sea beds of the Atlantic Ocean and the Pacific Ocean. Edmond Halley, *"An Account Of The Cause Of The Change Of The Variation Of The Magnetical Needle With An Hypothesis Of The Structure Of The Internal Parts Of The Earth"*, Philosophical Transactions, 16 (1692), p.563 to 587. The paper was read to the Royal Society on the 25 November 1691, and was officially published on the 4 March 1692.

On the 4 March 1692 Edmond Halley the discoverer of Halleys Comet, was the first to put forth the concept that the Planet Earth was comprised of layered concave shells. But over the years, the mainstream media view took precedence and majority of evidence has always supported the Planet Earth having a molten core, which geological substances are layered around.

After many years the Hollow Earth Theory of Sir Edmond Halley and John Cleves Symmes were brought to public attention and were given consideration and some kind of validity, because the United States Department of the Navy organised the flight of Lieutenant Commander Richard Evelyn Byrd and Chief Aviation Pilot Floyd Bennett to the North Polar Region on the 9 May 1926. The claim of Lieutenant Commander Richard Evelyn Byrd verified by the National Geographic Society.

There are only a few diagrams which have been produced to explain the basics of the Hollow Earth Theory. Within the book called The Hollow Earth, written by Walter Isidor Siegmeister, who became more commonly known as Doctor Raymond Walter Bernard, was used by him to explain how the Planet Earth is a geological shell that is 802 miles (1,290 KM) thick and in the North Polar Region and South Polar Region there are entrances which are 1,403 miles (2,258 KM) in diameter. So anybody individual or contingent that sailed into those entrances would not actually realise they would be entering the Hollow Earth, because of the gradual curvatures. Do entrances in the North Polar Region and the South Polar Region actually exist?
In the United Kingdom, the Green Children of Woolpit has become a traditional story, which is about a brother

and sister who were described as Green Children. They appeared in the village of Woolpit, that is midst the towns of Bury Saint Edmunds and Stowmarket. Much of English Folklore in this area of Central Suffolk, and elsewhere across East Anglia, mentions the hauntings in the meadows and fields around the villages of Wetherden, Borley Green, Woolpit, Drinkstone, Tostock and Elmswell. During the 25 August 1146, whilst King Stephen Blois or King Stephen The First, ruled England, a couple of Green Children suddenly appeared in the village of Woolpit. None of the villagers could explain where the Green Children had originated from, as they seem to materialise from absolutely nowhere. However, the Green Children mentioned they had been walking in a luminescent meadow, and then heard the sound of bells chiming, just before the Green Children then appeared in the village of Woolpit. Both the Green Children spoke with an unusual dialect and intonation patterns. Seemingly the infants had been somehow transported from inside Planet Earth to the countryside of Central Suffolk, in England.

Both of the Green Children had come from a Twilight World where the Sun never shone, and everything was luminescent. Apparently the area of the Hollow Earth which the Green Children came from was verdant and radiantly shimmered. Both of the Green Children mentioned that the location they had resided in was called Saint Martin's Land. From what the Green Children stated, it seems they had travelled from a located in the Hollow Earth.

Many generations ago, there were fertile meadows in North Staffordshire which an Englishman by the name of Jonathan Edmund Hemsworth, regularly maintained. During the 15 June 1704 he had been digging a trench for drainage purposes. Whilst he was clearing soil Jonathan Edmund Hemsworth discovered a large iron plate, that was oval shaped. On the topside of the iron plate was a mounted iron ring. He pulled the iron ring, and the plate made a scraping noise as it opened. Jonathan Edmund Hemsworth looked down into a vast depth and observed what appeared to be a set of dusty looking stairs which had been carved into the rock walls. The stairs led downwardly into an entrance which linked with subterranean passageways. It is believed the location in which Jonathan Edmund Hemsworth found the entrance was the Dimmingsdale Valley, near to the village of Alton, in North Staffordshire.

Although the only clue that was initially given for the location showed it was a meadow in an elongated rural area, that was surrounded by woodlands. This story can be found in 'A History Of Staffordshire' by the English Naturalist, Doctor Robert Plot, who wrote the book in 1709.

The adventurous Norseman called Olaf Jansen was born in the seafaring resort of Oulu, which is also known as Uleåborg. Such a seaside town is situated in the expanse of North Ostrobothnia in Central Finland, on the easterly coastline of the Gulf of Bothnia. For many years in this northerly area of the Baltic Sea, Olaf Jansen learned about sailing and fishing. When he was born on the 27 October 1811, both the parents of Olaf Jansen were on a fishing cruise on the Gulf of Bothnia, within Eastern Sweden and Western Finland.

The story of Olaf Jansen and his father, Jens Jansen, is famously told in *The Smoky God, Or A Voyage Journey To The Inner Earth,* that is a book that Willis George Emerson wrote in 1908. The story is about Olaf Jansen and his father who in 1829, sailed from Stockholm, in South Eastern Sweden and drifted towards the North Polar Region, and the entered into the Hollow Earth. Both Olaf Jansen and his father, Jens Jansen, were apparently greeted by 12 feet tall Nordic Giants who reside in the Hollow Earth, where they lived for two years. The fruits and vegetables seemingly grew to huge sizes in the Crystal Cities of the Hollow Earth, and therefore across the etheric landscapes were large grapes, oranges and peaches which thrived everywhere, because of the electromagnetic frequencies and vibrations that emanated from misty looking Central Sun. Both Olaf Jansen and Jens Jansen rode in a wireless form of public transport and lived amongst the Aryan Giants whose life spans lasted for over 800 years. *The Smoky God, Or A Voyage Journey To The Inner Earth*, is a beautiful story that is full of many twists and turns. When Olaf Jansen and Jens Jansen returned to the surface of Planet Earth, and he mentioned what had transpired, Olaf Jansen was placed into a mental asylum for 28 years. It was only on his death bed that Olaf Jansen felt he could actually tell his story.

There have been many contingents from the U.S. Navy which have explored both the North Polar Region and South Pole Region. Such activities began when Captain Charles David Wilkes, commanded the United States Exploring Expedition for the U.S. Navy, and reached the Antarctic Continent on the 16 January 1840, where further coastlines were then sighted on the 25 January 1840. On the 9 May 1926, Lieutenant Commander Richard Evelyn Byrd of the U.S. Navy and Chief Aviation Pilot Floyd Bennett, attempted a flight over the North Pole in a Fokker F7A 3M tri-motor monoplane named Josephine Ford. The monoplane had been named after the daughter of the Edsel Bryant Ford, who was the President of the Ford Motor Company, as that company helped to finance the Arctic Expedition. The flight left from Spitsbergen and returned to there, after both of them had journeyed for 15 hours and 57 minutes, which included 13 minutes spent circling at the Farthest North. Both Lieutenant Commander Richard Evelyn Byrd and Chief Aviation Pilot Floyd Bennett said they reached the North Pole.

After this flight had been completed Lieutenant Commander Richard Evelyn Byrd then led the First Antarctic Expedition, that was also called the Byrd Antarctic Expedition 1 (BAE 1). The First Antarctic Expedition was a reconnaissance flight mission which began on the 22 August 1928 and ended on the 18 June 1930. He was made a Rear Admiral by the United States Congress on the 21 December 1929. Therefore, as a newly appointed Rear Admiral, the adventurous Richard Evelyn Byrd then led the Second Antarctic Expedition, which occurred between the 16 March 1934 to the 17 October 1934. Whilst he explored the Antarctic Continent, Rear Admiral Richard Evelyn Byrd actually founded the First Antarctic Lodge Number 777 of the New Zealand Constitution on the 5 February 1935. He also invented his own Masonic Order, and called it the Order Of The Penguin. What is also interesting to note is how Rear Admiral Richard Evelyn Byrd led the Second Antarctic Expedition, with mainly individuals who were members of Masonic Lodges, as 60 of the 82 members were Scottish Rite Freemasons.

Only when Rear Admiral Richard Evelyn Byrd and Task Force 68 led the Fourth Antarctic Expedition, which became defined as Operation Highjump, from the 31 December 1946 to the 15 February 1947, did he encounter the Vierte Reiches Kriegsmarine (Fourth Empire Warfare Navy) and the Vierte Reiches Raumflotte (Fourth Empire Space Fleet), which had been covertly inhabited the Antarctic Continent since the 7 February 1934.

The huge convoy was comprised of the USS Mount Olympus (AGC-8), the aircraft carrier USS Philippine Sea (CG-58) and the 13 support vessels, which had been assembled for Operation Highjump. With swift determination the convoy arrived in the Ross Sea, which is located just off the coastline of South Western Antarctica, on the 31 December 1946. Once the convoy arrived various aerial explorations of an area half the size of the United States, were carried out. The Antarctic Expedition was terminated abruptly on the 15 February 1947, around 6 months earlier than scheduled, and the entire contingent returned to the United States of America. Even though the USS Mount Olympus (AGC-8) and the 13 support vessels returned to the United States on that date, it is believed the aircraft carrier USS Philippine Sea (CG-58) sailed by the Antarctic Peninsula and far out into the Weddell Sea, but did not return to the United States until the 25 February 1947.

Because he carried out so many excursions to the Arctic Continent and the Antarctic Continent, Rear Admiral Richard Evelyn Byrd established quite a reputation for himself in the U.S. Navy. He was known to be a very brave, kind and honest man, who was liked and respected. Rear Admiral Richard Evelyn Byrd was designated with commanding Operation Highjump, which started on the 31 December 1946 and ended on the 15 February 1947. The official story that was given as the reason for Operation Highjump, was to establish a Research Station. However, if anyone delves into this story, it becomes clear that a lot more was actually going on, because the Office of Naval Intelligence in Washington DC knew about the advanced Occult Technology which the Viertes Reich (Fourth Empire) had manufactured. Hence, it became obvious that over a long duration the Nazional Sozialistische Deutsche Arbeiter Partei, NSDAP (National Socialist German Workers Party, NSGWP), had been covertly transporting substantial quantities of equipment to the South Polar Region.

After returning from Operation Highjump, Rear Admiral Richard Evelyn Byrd then planned to charter a flight to the North Polar Region. Hence, on the 18 February 1947, he arrived on the Arctic Continent. Once there, Rear Admiral Richard Evelyn Byrd left Base Camp Arctic and flew northward on the 19 February 1947. What actually happened on that bizarre flight? For years rumours have persisted that on his historic flight to the Arctic Continent, Rear Admiral Richard Evelyn Byrd flew beyond the North Polar Region into an entrance which coursed into the Hollow Earth. Whilst there, Rear Admiral Richard Evelyn Byrd apparently encountered the Extraterrestrials known as the Nordic Aldebarians, who conveyed a very sobering message to him, which they want him to deliver to other Human Beings upon the Surface World. He wrote a navigation log and diary which he used to write about the unusual trees, plants, and mammals he observed upon the Arctic Continent. Rear Admiral Richard Evelyn Byrd even observed what appeared to be a Mammoth. He even claimed to have met with Nordic Aryans that were either Germans or some kind of Extraterrestrials who appeared to be Aryans. When Rear Admiral Richard Evelyn Byrd stated *"I'd Like To See That Land Beyond The Pole, It's The*

Centre Of The Great Unknown," he was obviously inferring that on the Arctic Continent was an entrance into the Hollow Earth.

Upon his return to Washington DC, on the 11 March 1947, Rear Admiral Richard Evelyn Byrd was interviewed over many hours by Intelligence Specialists from the Office of Naval Intelligence and Navy Physicians from the Medical Corps of the U. S. Navy, concerning what had transpired during Operation Highjump and the encounter which Rear Admiral Richard Evelyn Byrd had experienced with the Nordic Aldebarians at the North Polar Region.

We are told that Planet Earth is solid, but no discernible confirmation has ever been given which could then be used to confirm whether that assumption is true or not. When the Soviet Union drilled the Kolskaya Sverkhglubokaya Skvazhina (Kola Superdeep Borehole), that was also called SG-3A, the intention was to explore various kinds of geological strata beneath the Kola Peninsula and the Pechengsky District of the Murmansk Oblast, in North Western Russia. This objective was seen as a scientific attempt to drill as deep as possible into the crust of Planet Earth, whilst different geological substances could be examined. The drilling of the Kola Superdeep Borehole started on 24 May 1970, and the drilling rigs of Uralmash-4E and Uralmash-15000 series were used for this purpose. Hence, by using this equipment, the Soviet Union ensured the Kola Superdeep Borehole would become the deepest artificially excavated entry point on Planet Earth, which eventually reached a depth of 40,230 feet or 12,262 metres, which in terms of other units of length, is 7.6 miles (12.7 KM). The drilling was stopped on the 5 August 1994. Because the geological crust around the

Hollow Earth is 802.5 miles (1,291.5 KM) thick, once the drilling had been completed, the entry point had only reached a miniscule depth into the mantle of Planet Earth.

After the famous explorer known as Steve Currey, from the city of Provo, in Northern Utah, scheduled and organised his trip which he called 'Voyage To Our Hollow Earth,' he garnered a lot of public attention. This individual had offered the 'Voyage To Our Hollow Earth,' for 20,000 U.S. Dollars, and the excursion to the North Polar Region was scheduled for the 26 June 2007 to the 19 July 2007. Steve Currey claimed he would take anyone into the Hollow Earth and explained what the trip would entail. Because Steve Currey developed serious medical conditions, he unfortunately had to cancel the excursion to the Hollow Earth, and passed away on the 15 October 2007.

Numerous indications have been given which reveal where possible entrances into the Hollow Earth are located, and these include the Himalayas, the Tian Shan Mountains and the Altai Mountains. Additionally, the Tora Bora (Black Cave), which is in the Spin Ghar (White Mountains) of Eastern Afghanistan, Mount Shasta at the southerly end of the Cascade Range in Siskiyou County, Northern California, and there are likewise many others.

In the Sanskrit Language the landmasses of the Hollow Earth are called Agārtha (Shining Land), which is an etheric location that is also known by the name of Asgārtha (Shining Land). Over many generations the Buddhists from India, Nepal, Bhutan and Tibet, have likewise called the etheric location Agārtta (Shining Land), Aghārti (Shining Land), Agārath (Shining Land), Aghārta (Shining Land), Agārta (Shining Land) and

Agārttha (Shining Land). Some individuals believe the Hollow Earth resonates beyond spacetime, and therefore it is a location which is completely invisible unless the observer starts to psychically shift their own frequencies and vibrations. Maybe Olaf Jansen and Jens Jansen entered that altered state because they both spent so much time sailing on the Norwegian Sea and the Arctic Ocean, before entering into the Hollow Earth, where they were able to discernibly perceive the etheric landscapes and interact with the inhabitants.

Another interesting fact about the Antarctic Continent is that the landmass has no population of Humans. This landmass in the North Polar Region is called a political territory which means it is a condominium. When the Antarctic Treaty was signed on the 1 December 1959 by dignitaries from 12 countries in Washington DC, it was created to ensure the North Polar Region would be used as a scientific reserve. However, the Antarctic Treat of today is now comprised of 56 countries who have pledged to use the landmass for the same reason. Because of this purpose, the Antarctic Treaty System (ATS) was administered by the United Nations (UN), so they could equally share the management of the Antarctic Continent among the countries who had signed the Antarctic Treaty. All these countries have established Research Stations on the Antarctic Continent. Why have so many countries made a geopolitical pact and come together in this vast expanse? Why are civilian flights prohibited from flying over the Antarctic Continent, if these 56 countries are only using the landmass as a scientific reserve?

Doctor Raymond Bernard postulated that within the geological crust of Planet Earth, there was a Central Sun. Additionally, he believed that planets and moons in the Solar System all contained interior life because they had cavernous and spacious interiors. The electromagnetic resonances of the Aurora Borealis (North Wind Dawn) and the Aurora Australis (South Wind Dawn) are supposedly the photons that radiate from the Central Sun, which then chemically react with the atmosphere of Planet Earth. Apparently the Hollow Earth has clear blue skies and mountainous locations that upwardly extend over 10 miles and more. This information does seem like a scene in a movie from Hollywood.

Because the Dalai Blama (Large Chief Priest) was given the spiritual name Jetsun Jamphel Ngawang Lobsang Yeshe Tenzin Gyatso. He would also eventually become known as Tenzin Gyatso, and this meant he was appointed to become the knowledge protector of the Hollow Earth. This individual was born Lhamo Thondup, and is commonly known as Gyalwa Rinpoche to the Tibetan People. For them, he is the collectively respected 14th Dalai Lama, who has a profound awareness of the Chushel Rgyalkhag (Crystal Kingdom), which resonates beyond spacetime, and is an etheric location that also became defined as the Chushel Gyekhap (Crystal Kingdom). Such an environment is likewise called the Bikraba Rgyalkhag (Shining Kingdom) of the Bidebyung (Silence Place), which intensely sparkles and radiates inside the Hollow Earth.

According to the discreet beliefs of the Dalai Lama and Tibetan Folklore, the numerous Chushel Phugpa (Crystal Caves) and Olasa Khungbupa (Underground Tunnels), which lead into the Kyong Sachha (Hollow Earth), are part of the etheric Olasa Jikten (Underground World). Such resplendent expanses course directly beneath the Tibetan Plateau, which is also called the Qinghai Tibet Plateau, the Qing Zang Plateau and the Himalayan Plateau, of Eastern Asia.

Even though the Buddhist Temples which exist across the Tibet Autonomous Region are managed by the religious communities of Nangpa Trapa (Enlightened Monks), whose collective awareness of the Hollow Earth, is kept away from the public. Indeed, the devoutly religious Tampa Blamapa (Sacred High Priests), who are likewise defined as the Gapu Blamapa (Elder High Priests) and the Chhonden Blamapa (Pious High Priests), continue to keep their knowledge of the Hollow Earth away from the Tibetan People because they realise how profound the residents of the Hollow Earth really are.

Some aspects of Tibetan Folklore, mention that beneath the Potala Palace and the city of Lhasa, in Eastern Tibet, are linked Öchhempo Jangkhu Khungbupa (Luminous Green Tunnels) and Sangwa Khungbupa (Secret Tunnels), which extend downwardly into the Hollow Earth. Many of the Buddhist Monks are privately aware of the shimmering Chushel Khrompa (Crystal Cities) which the World King psychically rules over. From those etheric settlements he perpetually helps to unify the Chhempo Gyappa Rigyü (Great Shining Nation), whilst the somewhat translucent Chushel Gyekhappa (Crystal Kingdoms) brightly resonate beyond spacetime. Behind the closed doors of the Buddhist Temples the religious lineage of the Pöpa Blamapa (Tibetan High Priests) has been used to protect their supernal knowledge about the Odchenpo Migyü (Radiant People), who they also define as the Odgsal Migyü (Luminous People), which are individuals who apparently inhabit the Hollow Earth.

Because the concept of a Hollow Earth is not taught in schools, colleges and universities, the majority of Humans never focus on the idea that inside Planet Earth are civilisations which exist beyond spacetime. Indeed, the essence of the Hollow Earth Theory is actually connected with the collective spiritual development of Humans, and symbolises our profound awareness of the self. As the author of the Conversations With God books, Neal Donald Walsch, said *"If You Don't Go Within, You Go Without."* This is exactly what has occurred with the thinking of Humans, as the Elites and their Secret Societies continue to hide the scientific truths about the actual structure of Planet Earth.

We must remember that it is the duty of Humans to explore and discover the supernatural because this will help us to integrally develop and learn more about the unseen aspects of Planet Earth. It is a sobering to realise that we know more about the structure of the Moon than we do about the vast depths of the Atlantic Ocean and the Pacific Ocean. Have these deviated perspectives been deliberately created to prevent Humans from gaining a wider discernment of actuality? Even though it is feasible that the Hollow Earth is an expanse which is actually etheric, and therefore resonates beyond spacetime, it is highly unlikely that Planet Earth is a completely solid geological structure. There are so many stories about the Hollow Earth, that in some form or another they officially represent information which does not make sense. Hence, would any of you ever consider visiting the Hollow Earth?

CHAPTER 8: BREAKAWAY CIVILISATIONS

Any civilisation that has individuals who have covertly gained access to advanced technologies will eventually diverge from the previous societal conventions. Hence, it is believed this same process has transpired on Planet Earth. Many events have occurred in the last 75 years which have contributed towards the covert development of a breakaway civilisation. For example, on the 14 October 1936 a spacecraft was retrieved in Germany, that was covertly retrieved and studied, before its components were exploited in the manufacturing of advanced spacecraft. Once the U.S. Department of the Army created and used Operation Paperclip, to bring scientists from National Socialist Germany to the United States of America, from the 16th July 1945 and onward to the 31 October 1959, another move had been made towards a breakaway civilisation becoming actualised. When this happened the progression of societies paths would have split. Then once the Greada Treaty was established in the United States of America on the 20 February 1954, another phase had also been achieved. This is certainly going the step beyond and accepting some bitter truth about everything we have been educated to believe in schools, colleges and universities, but all this information is publicly accessible and for you to make your own mind up. We are collecting information and research and leaving it for you to decide.

The idea of Humans existing in the Solar System with technologies which are not commercially available for public usage, was aptly described on the 23 April 815 AD when the Catholic Priest who was known as Archbishop Abogard Valtierra, wrote a treatise about Weather Magic called *De Grandine Et Tonitruis* (On Hail

And Thunder). In that treatise Bishop Abogard Valtierra wrote a few paragraphs about airships which descend from the Nubes Regni (Cloud Realm) or the Royaume Nuages (Cloud Realm), whose sailors were thought to take fruits, vegetable and other crops which had been damaged by hailstorms, back to Magonia (Having Power Country). Whilst he resided in the city of Lyon, which is located in the Auvergne Rhône Alpes Region of Eastern France, Archbishop Abogard Valtierra wrote his fascinating treatise. The etheric residency was called Magonia (Having Power Country), and was the Cloud Realm where the inhabitants were said to travel through the sky in airships. Sometimes they would occasionally invite some Humans from the Planet Earth up to their Cloud Realm.

During the 14 October 1936 a contingent of Sicherheitspolizei (Security Police) discovered and retrieved a crashed alien spacecraft from the Schwarzwald (Black Forest) of Baden-Württemberg in South Western Germany. The crashed spacecraft was removed and stored in the city of Heidelberg. While the upheaval of World War 2 was happening, the National Socialist Germans were looking into interdimensional travel, reverse engineering alien spacecraft and searching for prehistoric esoteric knowledge to Planet Earth. Professor Winfried Otto Schumann from the Technical University, Munich, and the incredible Austrian Croat who was a psychic known as Maria Oršitsch, were both were asked to study the crashed alien spacecraft, and once they had completed their inspection of it, the Sicherheitspolizei (Security Police) then removed the spacecraft and transported it on the 15th December 1936, to the Eisenbahnkaserne (Railway Barracks) and the Luftschifferkaserne (Airship Barracks), in the city of

Munich, where the Reichswehr (Empire Defense) took over the supervision and protection of the spacecraft.

The elegant and intriguing Austrian Croat psychic called Maria Oršitsch who founded the Alledeutschen Gesellschaft Für Metaphysik (All German Society For Metaphysics) during the 15 April 1921, did so because she had apparently been guided by the Nordic Aldebarians to create the organisation, so that psychically received information could be discreetly archived, studied and effectively used. She eventually called her organisation, the Vril Gesellschaft (Vital Force Society). to explore the origins of the Aryan People, to seek contact with the Verborgene Meister (Hidden Masters) of Ultima Thule, and to practice meditation techniques that were intended to strengthen individual mastery of the Vrilkraft (Vital Force Power).

During the 17 December 1923, the psychically received information about the interstellar spacecraft that became known as the Jenseitsflugmaschine, JFM (Other World Flying Device, OWFD), was meticulously recorded by Maria Oršitsch. However, the actual manufacturing of the Other World Flying Device, from consistently looking at the diagrams which Maria Oršitsch had created, was not such an easy task.

The psychical transmissions which Maria Oršitsch claimed she had received from the Arianische Leute (Light Deity People), that were also definable called the Ariannische Leute (Light Deity People), and the "Leichte Gottheitswesen" ("Light Deity Beings"). From what has become shown, it appears that the Light Deity People were the Nordic Aldebarians, who apparently reside on planets and moons in the Alpha Tauri Solar System of the stellar mass called Alpha Tauri and Aldebaran. This stellar mass is located in the Taurus Constellation, and shimmers around 72 lights years from Planet Earth. With concise proficiency, the Nordic Aldebarians psychically conveyed information to Maria Oršitsch which contained technical data and precise instructions on how to proficiently manufacture the Other World Flying Device.

Maria Oršitsch and the other Vrilen Damen (Vital Force Ladies), that were sometimes named the Vrilerinnen (Vital Force Stream), started to psychically received even more schematic information concerning how to manufacture interstellar Überisch Flugmaschinen (Super Flying Devices), that would become the Flugscheiben (Flying Disks) and the Fliegende Räder (Flying Wheels) of the Third Reich. Eventually, both the Thule Gesellschaft (Northern Society) and Vril Gesellschaft (Vital Force Society), covertly benefited from the psychically received information on how to construct different kinds of spacecraft.

From around the 18 April 1932, and then onward during World War 2, convoys of vessels that had become defined as the Wehrmacht Kriegsmarine Unterseebooten (Armed Forces Warfare Navy Submarines), were sent from National Socialist Germany to the Antarctic Continent. Many of the Super Flying Devices, such as the Flying Disks and the Flying Wheels, were then covertly manufactured at the North Polar Region.

Once the convoy deliveries had been completed, the National Socialist Germans managed to effectively conceal their aeronautic technologies in the Luftwaffe Raumschiff Einrichtungen, LRE (Airspace Weapon Spaceship Installations, AWSI), that were likewise called the Luftwaffe Raumfahrzeuge Einrichtungen, LRE (Airspace Weapon Spacecraft Installations, AWSI), which they had constructed from the 24 April 1932.

Hence, the location called Neuschwabenland, within North Eastern Antarctic, became a very important area for the Third Reich as they were able to use the glacial landscape to hide the construction of their advanced Tiefe Unterirdische Soldatisch Festungen, TUSF (Deep Underground Military Fortresses, DUMF). With similar classification, such facilities also became defined as the Tiefe Unterirdische Kriegerisch Festungen, TUKF (Deep Underground Military Fortresses, DUMF).

Professor Winfried Otto Schumann, who was employed at the Technical University, in the city of Munich, in the Free State of Bavaria, Southern Germany, and the incredible Austrian Croat who was a psychic known as Maria Oršitsch, who became the Vrilleiter (Vital Force Director) of the Vril Gesellschaft (Vital Force Society), began to study the retrieved alien spacecraft on the 14 October 1936, for the Drittes Reich (Third Empire) of Germany. The very first German Astronaut to land on the Moon was Kapitänleutnant Werner Theisenberg of the Kriegsmarine (Warfare Navy), on the 23 August 1942.

Werner Norbert Theisenberg specifically landed on the Mare Imbrium, within the Imbrium Basin of the Moon. After the National Socialist Germans established a permanent scientific facility on the Moon, the manufacturing of Flying Disks then became their priority. Many advancements in Occult Technology were built, but the Raumkreuzer (Space Cruisers) were manufactured using the reverse engineered alien spacecraft, they became the Dunkle Flotte (Dark Fleet) of the Fourth Reich. Adolf Hitler even a did a trip in search of the Hollow Earth. Like always World War 2 was just a smoke screen to keeping Humans distracted while other objectives and missions were carried through.

The famous director of movies, known as Stanley Kubrick filmed the landings on the Moon for the Project Apollo, which became the Apollo Program. We have been told that NASA landed Neil Alden Armstrong and Edwin Eugene Aldrin Junior, better known as Buzz Aldrin, on the Moon during the 20 July 1969. Well, whatever your beliefs are, there is evidence that all the events did actually happen.

On the 16 July 1945 Operation Paperclip became a transference process which the Joint Chiefs of Staff at the U.S. War Department, and eventually the U.S. Defense Department, collectively established, where over 1,500 German Scientists, Engineers, and Technicians from National Socialist Germany to the United States of America for employment. Where many scientific endeavours were developed and the Secret Space Program (SSP) covertly began.

"I Think That There Are A Number Of Anomalous Events We Know Have Occurred In Earth Orbit And Beyond Earth Orbit. We've Got 40 Years Of Events Recorded By U.S. And Soviet Astronauts Of Objects In Orbit That Appear To Be Not Our Own That Seemed To Move Intelligently." - Richard Michael Dolan.

Substantial research about the subject of UFO sightings, Ultraterrestrials and Extraterrestrials, has been done over the past 75 years and Richard Dolan is an individual who has established his credibility when it comes this subject. According to Richard Dolan, satellites from the Defense Support Program (DSP) which had been created and managed by 460th Space Wing of the U.S. Air Force, were used to detect the spacecraft of Extraterrestrials, after the Integrated Missile Early Warning Satellite 1 (IMEWS-1) was on launched into orbit during the 6 November 1970. Hence, between October 1973 to December 1991, the Defense Support Program (DSP) detected 298 alien spacecraft. So where do these covert interstellar civilisations exist? What is the purpose of these covert interstellar civilisations?

According to the eminent data scientist known as Edward Twietmeyer, much of the Planet Mars was occupied in the distant past and has become occupied again in the present. Within his October 2005 book, called *What NASA Isn't Telling You About Mars*, Edward Twietmeyer confirms these facts.

With these kinds of discoveries, the spacecraft known as Clementine and the Deep Space Program Science Experiment (DSPSE), also revealed that numerous alien structures exist on the Moon, which has seemingly become occupied in recent times. Clementine was jointly developed by the Ballistic Missile Defense Organization (BMDO) and the National Aeronautics and Space Administration (NASA), and was launched on the 25 January 1994. After getting to the Moon, Clementine entered into orbit during the 19 February 1994. Whilst in orbit around the Moon, the spacecraft photographed numerous alien structures, such as transparent domes, metallic spacecraft and geometric mechanisms. Some of the angular looking mechanisms were also seen moving about on the unusual terrain of the Moon. The alien structures were even featured in the March 2010 book, *Lunar Orbiter Photographic Atlas Of The Near Side Of The Moon,* written by the systems engineer, known as Charles James Byrne.

Midst the remote expanse of the S-4 Base, which is located at Papoose Lake, near to the Papoose Range of South Eastern Nevada, dimensional portals have supposedly been constructed. Because the S-4 Base is located southward of Area 51, in the area called Lincoln County and the Great Basin Desert, then it might well be the case that in this part of South Eastern Nevada, dimensional portals are regularly used by the Military Industrial Complex (MIC) to covertly transport equipment and supplies to the Planet Mars and the dark side of the Moon. If you look at The Phildelphia Experiment, which apparently happened on the 28 October 1943, you can easily discern how such dimensional portals effectively function and resonate beyond spacetime. The former USAF Lieutenant Colonel, Donald Philips, went onto become an Aerospace Engineer who was employed by the Lockheed Martin Corporation. He testifies that we not only have spacecraft that were derived from Extraterrestrials, but have the U.S. Air Force has achieved tremendous technological advances from their study. Apparently, the North Atlantic Treaty Organisation (NATO) did research into the origin of Extraterrestrials, between April 1952 to October 1968, and the findings of their research were disseminated as detailed scientific reports to the 12 founding members who are Iceland, Norway, the United Kingdom of Great Britain, France, Luxembourg, Belgium, the Netherlands, Denmark, Italy, Portugal, Canada and the United States of America.

"The Knowledge I Have Of These Technologies Came From The Craft We Captured Here. I Didn't See The

Craft, Nor Did I See The Bodies, But I Certainly Knew Some Of The People That Did. There Was No Question That There Were Beings From Outside The Planet." - Donald Phillips, Lockheed Martin Corporation.

There are some very unusual situations that have happened over the last 30 years. During a 13 month duration, the individual who was born in Scotland, known as Gary McKinnon, was accused of cyber hacking into 97 computers at the U.S. Defense Department and the National Aeronautics and Space Administration (NASA), in the United States of America. Because of his expertise as a systems administrator, Gary McKinnon had become familiar with how to cyber hack into computer networks. The activities occurred between the 16 February 2001 and 8 March 2002, whilst Gary McKinnon was living in Palmers Green, in North London. He apparently hacked into the databases of the network systems which NASA use and then Gary McKinnon found a way to bypassing the normal kinds of encryption methods and authentication processes in the network systems at NASA. Once he had accomplished this, Gary McKinnon was then able to view classified documents and photographs of spacecraft and space stations of Solar Warden Space Fleet which the Naval Space Command (NSC) had been managing, that were apparently present in the Solar System.

Gary McKinnon found documents relating to interdimensional travel, photographs of huge spacecraft around Planet Earth and much more. But the biggest find was discovering there were servicemen from the U.S. Navy who were listed as Non-Terrestrial Officers (NTOs), that were designated with carrying out duties and tasks onboard spacecraft and space stations which do not orbit Planet Earth. After a very lengthy trial, the

U.S. Federal Government tried to extradite Gary McKinnon from his home in North London, to the United States of America.

Kerry Cassidy from Project Camelot, has done a lot of video interviews since 2004 which reveal a considerable amount of fascinating information from having conversations with individuals who have apparently been involved with the Secret Space Program (SSP) or were employed by the U.S. Army or the U.S. Marine Corps. Additionally, there have been individuals that worked for the U.S. Navy, U.S. Air Force, U.S. Space Force or the U.S. Coast Guard, who began to realise how the Military Industrial Complex (MIC) had established certain scientific and logistical arrangements with malevolent Extraterrestrials.

Has the entrepreneur called Elon Reeve Musk been designated to use Space X as a method to bridge the gap between the highly advanced breakaway civilisation and the mundane astronomical research of NASA? U.S. President Donald John Trump created the United States Space Force (USSF), the U.S. Navy released footage of UFO sightings, the pressure and control to bring in a World Government and a New World Order (NWO)? Are these events meant to prepare Humans for the next 10 years of the governance policies which the Elites and their Secret Societies have been planning for?

There have been trillions of U.S. Dollars which have been spent on covert operations over the last 75 years or more. Where has all that money actually gone? Why has no auditing been done to ascertain how the trillions of U.S. Dollars are spent? Are the controllers and manipulators now preparing for Humanity to accept the breakaway civilisation?

No one knows the exact truth and if they did, we still wouldn't know. But maybe the reason why the Elites and their Secret Societies contrived the Flat Earth Theory and Planet Dome Theory is to keep Humans continually distracted, so they do not focus on what is going on with the Secret Space Program (SSP) that is so prevalent in the Solar System. This kind of Occult Technology is so far beyond what we expect, and therefore most of it seems unimaginable. How would most Humans psychologically react to the mainstream media admitting that a breakaway civilisation exists in the Solar System and elsewhere in the Physical Universe?

CHAPTER 9: PREHISTORIC WARFARE

Although we have been told that nuclear warfare only became a realisation after World War 2 had ended and the Cold War was just beginning, this is not actually the case. Hence, nothing could be further from the truth. Even in the Holy Bible, we learn about the possible usage of prehistoric nuclear detonations. Within the Book of Genesis, it clearly states the following.

"Then The Lord Rained Upon Sodom And Upon Gomorrah Brimstone And Fire From The Lord Out Of Heaven; And He Overthrew Those Cities, And All The Plain, And All The Inhabitants Of The Cities, And That Which Grew Upon The Ground."

Genesis 19:24-19:25

There are numerous locations on Planet Earth where substantial quantities of pure silica quartz have been found. For example, in the Mojave Desert of South Eastern California, and elsewhere in the South Western United States, there appears to have been some kind of massive thermonuclear conflict that caused the sand to fuse and become pure silicon quartz. Whatever led to the nuclear conflict on Planet Earth, resulted in massive devastation, which occurred around 8,500 BC.

The engineer known as Albion William Hart, whilst employed at the Massachusetts Institute of Technology (MIT), did a scientific inspection of prehistoric silicon quartz and noticed the vast quantities of the substance were chemically identical to the chunks of glass or silicon dioxide left at the Trinity Site of the USAAF Alamogordo Bombing and Gunnery Range, in Southern New Mexico. Indeed, such an occurrence was also the case across similar arid locations of the South Western United States. This means that some kind of prehistoric nuclear conflict might have really happened, because radioactive glass or silicon dioxide has been found in the Thar Desert or the Great Indian Desert of North Western Indian, the Gobi Desert of Southern Mongolia and Northern China, in Eastern Asia, and in the Libyan Desert of North East Africa.

A huge area of strangely fused silica glass is buried across large depths of the Gobi Desert in Mongolia, Eastern Asia, where it is believed a massive city once existed. Other locations where slightly radioactive glass or silicon dioxide have been found, include the salt flat called Lop Nur or Lop Nor, which is situated on the edge of the Tarim Basin, in the Taklamakan Desert and the Kumtag Desert of South Eastern Xinjiang Province, in North Western China. Were there once numerous cities built in remote locations on Planet Earth, that were destroyed at the same time in a prehistoric nuclear conflict?

There are other wonders, such as the quantities of melted walls that shimmer with glittering blue glass, in the ruined city of Khara Khoto. Such walls were discovered at a depth of 1,850 metres by a Russian Archaeologist called Pyotr Kuzmich Kozlov, on the 16 October 1908. The glittering blue glass indicated that a vast nuclear conflict possible happened, and many of the ruins at Khara Khoto, were also found in the Helan Mountains, in the Ejin Banner of the Alxa League or Alashan League, in both Western Inner Mongolia and Northern China.

More than 70 prehistoric stone hillside forts in Scotland have vitrified walls where the stone has melted into glass after becoming exposed to intense heat that could only have come from some kind of a nuclear detonation. The Tap Onoth Hillfort, nearby the village of Rhynie, in North West Aberdeenshire, Scotland, is famous for its vitrified stone walls, that have been of fascination to visitors for a long time. The vitrified fortification which became known as called Dun Mac Sniachan among the Scottish Celtic Tribes. This fortification is located in in Argyll and Bute. Over subsequent generations the remnant building was given the name of Dun Mac Sniochain, Dun Mac Uisneachan, and Dun Mac Uisneadian. After the Roman Legions invaded Britain, the same location was called Beregonium and Berogomum, Upon the surfacing of Dun Mac Sniachan are stony pieces that contain glassy substances, which indicates the damage to the building could ony have occurred during some kind of the prehistoric nuclear conflict. Other famous examples can be found at the village of Benderloch, in Argyll and Bute, the resort town called Oban, in Argyll and Bute, Western Scotland, the forested hillside known as Craig Phadraig and Ord Hill, that is nearby to the village of North Kessock. Both these locations are both near to Inverness, in the Scottish Highlands, where a lot of supernatural activities happen on a regular basis.

The intense fascination with nuclear conflict was something that Julius Robert Oppenheimer wanted to explore further. Hence, after the attack by the Imperial Japanese Navy Air Service on Pearl Harbor, during the 7 December 1941, the U.S. Defense Department triggered the Manhattan Project, that was a covert weapons research program. One of the programs under the Manhattan Project was called Project Trinity, and was directed by the theoretical physicist, Julius Robert

Oppenheimer. He was dedicated to weaponizing nuclear fission as quickly as possible.

Julius Robert Oppenheimer was successful in achieving his objective. During the 16 July 1945, the United States Army Corps of Engineers (USACE) detonated a test plutonium bomb at the White Sands Proving Grounds, that is now called the White Sands Missile Range (WSMR), in the Tularosa Basin of the Great Basin Ranges. The communities of Manso Indians who reside around the Great Basin Ranges of the Chihuahuan Desert, in the South Western United States, have always emphasised the fact that unusual paranormal events occur in that location.

The explosion crater of the Trinity Site was 300 feet wide and 5 feet deep. Inside was a greenish looking, glassy substance that had temperatures of 3,090F or 1,700C, the minimum needed to melt silicon dioxide into glass. This radioactive glass was named 'Trinitite,' and was considered a unique substance that was not believed to exist anywhere else on Planet Earth.

Enthralled by the Bhagavad Gītā (Song From The Creator), the Vedic Hindu Indian Scripture that was written around 1,760 BC, Julius Robert Oppenheimer began Sanskrit Studies so he could read the text in the Sanskrit Language. While he was a professor, before to World War 2, he was known to quote numerous passages from the Mahābhārata (Great Being Maintained), which some researchers also similarly define as the Mahābhāratam (Great Being Maintained). He would do this in every class lecture. While much consideration is given to the Bhagavad Gītā (Song From The Creator), as a story, Julius Robert Oppenheimer, as a student and professor of theoretical physics and thermodynamics, was likely captivated by the explosive, burning weapons and devices that were described in detail, so precisely that modern researchers have been able to reverse engineer such technologies as part of the Military Industrial Complex (MIC).

One section of the Bhagavad Gītā (Song From The Creator), called the Droṇapannā (Bucket Book), which some academics likewise refer to as the Droṇakitāba (Bucket Book). Many communities of Hindu Indians also defined this document with the title of Droṇaśīṭa (Bucket Book), and Droṇapustaka (Bucket Book). This document specifically describes electromagnetic Āṣṭraḥ (Pointed Sticks) which could destroy entire armies, *"Causing Crowds Of Warriors With Steeds And Elephants And Weapons To Be Carried Away As If They Were Dry Leaves Of Trees."* Another weapon was described as producing vertical, billowing smoke clouds that opened consecutively like enormous canopies, reminiscent of the massive rising atomic clouds produced at the Trinity Site of the USAAF Alamogordo Bombing and Gunnery Range, in Southern New Mexico.

Among the most destructive Āṣtra (Pointed Stick) was the advanced device known as the Brahmāstra (Infinite Reality Pointed Stick), which had apparently been created by the Hindu Indian Deity called Brahma Ishvara. From what has been mentioned in the Hindu Scripture, the device was described as a *"Single Projectile Charged With All The Power In The Universe. It Was An Unknown Weapon, An Iron Thunderbolt, An Enormous Messenger Of Death Which Reduced To Ashes An Entire Race. There Was Neither A Counter Attack Nor A Defense That Could Stop It."*

The device known as the Āṣṭra (Pointed Stick) produced *"An Incandescent Column Of Smoke And Flame As Bright As 10,000 Solar Masses That Rose In All Its Splendor. After, Corpses Were So Burned As To Be Unrecognizable. Their Hair And Nails Fell Out; Pottery Broke Without Any Apparent Cause, And The Birds Turned A Whitish Hue. After A Few Hours, Foodstuffs Were Radioactively Contaminated And Infected."* Other indications were also given, which clearly revealed the destructive potential of these devices, because in the section of the Bhagavad Gītā, called the Droṇapannā, which is also known as the Droṇakitāba, and is similarly called the Droṇaśīṭa and the Droṇapustaka, it is mentions that *"Any Target Hit By The Brahmāstra (Infinite Reality Pointed Stick) Would Be Utterly Destroyed; Land Would Become Barren And Lifeless, Rainfall Would Cease, And Infertility In Humans And Animals Would Follow For Aeons Of Time."*

The powerful Brahmāstra (Infinite Reality Pointed Stick) was detonated at the end of the final 18 day conflict of Kurukshetra. Whilst this was going on, the Pāṇḍavaḥ (Pallid Ancestors) vanquished their enemy, the Kaurāvaḥ (Priest Ancestors), with the nuclear device, but the few surviving Pāṇḍavaḥ (Pallid Ancestors) discovered that there was nothing left to occupy, and no one left to rule. Seemingly, there were numerous Brahmāstraḥ (Infinite Reality Pointed Sticks) which had been used to destroy the community of Kaurāvaḥ and turned the Rājāsthān (Kings Place) or Rājāsthāna (Kings Place), into the radioactive Thar Desert or Great Indian Desert of North Western India.

Declassified accounts from observers that witnessed Project Trinity, correlate with the prehistoric descriptions of the weapon called the Brahmāstra (Infinite Reality

Pointed Stick). Such a device is mentioned in the Droṇapannā, which is a document that was also called the Droṇakitāba, Droṇaśīta and Droṇapustaka. Many fascinating insights are given in the writings of the Bhagavad Gītā (Song From The Creator), concerning the prehistoric nuclear conflict that occurred on Planet Earth. A witness that observed the nuclear detonation at the USAAF Alamogordo Bombing and Gunnery Range, was the physicist called Luis Walter Alvarez, who was sitting between the Pilot and First Officer of a Boeing B-29 Superfortress flying roughly 25 miles from the actual Trinity Test Site. Luis Walter Alvarez mentioned that *"Intense Light Covered My Field Of Vision, After Which I Noted An Orange Red Glow. The Cloud Started To Push Up."*

According to the U.S. Federal Government, the landmass called the White Sands Proving Ground, is a testing facility, which is located in parts of Dona Ana County. Because the covert testing area is also situated within Socorro County, and Otero County, Sierra County, and Lincoln County, in Southern New Mexico, large expanses of it are designated with restricted access. Some of those employed in the U.S. Federal Civil Service believed the area was mostly uninhabited. However, this was untrue, as there are numerous Mescalero Apache Indians who had dwellings there. Such gatherings of Native Americans sometimes reside on the Mescalero Apache Reservation, located in South Central New Mexico. Additionally, there are 42,000 Americans who live within the city of Alamogordo, in Otero County, Southern New Mexico. Numerous individuals observed the explosion and displayed health impacts shortly after the nuclear blast. Large swathes of crops, and livestock were also immediately contaminated.

A fascinating article was published in Popular Science, on the 20th August 1945. The article tells the story of Darryl Gilmore, from the village of Tularosa, in Otero County, Southern New Mexico, who was driving along Highway 380 near to the designated Trinity Test Site. The story mentions that Daryl Gilmore was driving home from Albuquerque, in Bernalillo County, and then onward across North Central New Mexico, during the morning of the 16 July 1945. He said that he did not observe the nuclear flash emanating from the USAAF Alamogordo Bombing and Gunnery Range, in Southern New Mexico, before he left. However, numerous Ground Infantry (GI) from the United States Army Corps of Engineers (USACE), were seen by him on Highway 380. They told him to roll up his windows, as there were poison gases in the area. Soon after, his arms, neck, and face turned sunburn red. Daryl Gilmore stated that his *"Outer Skin Gradually Fell Off"* and that *"A Few Years Later"* he began to have *"Skin Problems."*

The crash of the spacecraft became known as the Padilla Ranch UFO Incident, which allegedly happened the same year as Project Trinity occurred, in the Tularosa Basin of the Chihuahuan Desert, midst Southern New Mexico. When Project Trinity was activated by detonation of a nuclear device on the 16 July 1945, did the United States Army Corps of Engineers (USACE), do this so they could act out some kind of ritual, to open up a pathway into locations in the Physical Universe or alternate dimensions?

The nuclear detonation at the USAAF Alamogordo Bombing and Gunnery Range was part of the Manhattan Project that ended Word War 2 with the atomic bombing on the 6 August 1945 of the city known as Hiroshima. Exuded uranium radiation then spread across the Hiroshima Prefecture of the Chūgoku Region, on Honshu Island in Central Japan. During the 9 August 1945, the atomic bombing of Nagasaki occurred. Just as with Hiroshima, massive amount of uranium radiation spread and contaminated the Nagasaki Prefecture of Kyushu Island, in Southern Japan. Whilst the atomic bombing happened, round shaped metallic spacecraft were seen hovering near to the devastated cities in Japan.

When the nuclear detonation was activated on the USAAF Alamogordo Bombing and Gunnery Range, various kinds of UFO sightings arose from the event. Were they drawn to this area of Southern New Mexico because of Project Trinity? Additionally, it is also known that whenever nuclear detonations occur, massive lightning storms will then start to happen. This is because the flumes of radioactive uranium or plutonium dust becomes diffused into the atmosphere, where they cause unusual electrochemical reactions.

According to Jose Padilla, Remigio Baca and Sabrina Padilla, who were resident of South New Mexico, a very unusual looking UFO crashed on the Padilla Ranch, in the Census Designated Place (CDP) of San Antonio, on the 13 August 1945. Many UFO sightings had occurred across Socorro County, in Central New Mexico, but this UFO actually crashed. Because the Tularosa Basin of the Chihuahuan Desert, in Southern New Mexico, is directly adjacent to San Antonio, it is believed that many of the UFO sightings are connected with the supernatural activities which the Mescalero Apache Indians have stated are a regular occurrence there.

Jose Padilla, Remigio Baca and Sabrina Padilla say the United States Army Air Forces (USAAF) concealed evidence about the metallic round shaped UFO, which crashed onto the Padilla Ranch during a massive lightning storm on the 13 August 1945. Did the United States Army Air Forces (USAAF) know more about the UFO and its occupants? Was the UFO crash somehow linked with the nuclear detonation ritual at the USAAF Alamogordo Bombing and Gunnery Range?

The investigative journalist and UFO researcher, Paola Leopizzi Harris, and the Internet pioneer, computer scientist, astronomer, venture capitalist and UFO researcher, Jacques Fabrice Vallee, teamed up to uncover the details of the alleged UFO crash that occurred in the Chihuahuan Desert. Their research was placed into a book called Trinity: The Best Kept Secret. Both of the investigators have provided witness accounts of how the United States Army Air Forces (USAAF) intercepted a UFO and certain Extraterrestrials, that were piloting the spacecraft, on the 13 August 1945.

Paola Leopizzi Harris and Jacques Fabrice Vallee claim to have documented evidence of a tapered oval shaped UFO weighing 72 tons which had been removed from the Padilla Ranch, in the Census Designated Place (CDP) of San Antonio, where it crash landed on the 13 August 1945. Where did the oval shaped UFO actually come from? Was it piloted by Extraterrestrials or were the occupants artificially created lifeforms?

Around 10 miles westward from the city of Jodhpur, in Northern Rajasthan, midst North Western India, there is a 3 square mile radioactive zone that was discovered whilst an excavation was going on for residential construction purposes. Below the surface were circular patterned layers of highly radioactive dust and ashes, "*Consistent With What Occurs Underneath A Typical Air Burst Nuclear Detonation.*" The construction of housing in that area of Jodhpur was cancelled. However, in 2016, the Defence Minister, known as Manohar Parrikar, ordered the Defense Research and Development Organization (DRDO) mades plans at his premises in Calcutta or New Delhi, to construct a scientific facility at Jodhpur, where drone mounted radioactivity sensors could be produced. Was there a prior knowledge concerning the prehistoric nuclear conflict which occurred at Jodhpur? Why would the Defense Research and Development Organization plan such a facility, in the National Capital Territory (NCT) of Delhi, in North Western India? Did Manohar Parrikar know more about the prehistoric nuclear conflict? What is it relevant to use Jodhpur for this scientific purpose?

After the ruins of Harappa, in the Sahiwal District of Punjab Province, in Central Eastern Pakistan, were discovered in 1912, the radiation levels were found to be very high there. Some distance from Harappa, is the prehistoric city of Mohenjo Daro (Deceased People Mound), located in the Larkana District of the Sindh Province, in South Eastern Pakistan. The ruins were discovered in 1922. Again, high radiation levels seem to be present in that location. Both the sites were dated to around 2,530 BC. Once archaeological excavation began, and the personnel reached the original street levels, they found 44 skeletons sprawled in the prehistoric roadways. The educational administrator from America, known as David Davenport, found what would have been a large blast epicenter, "*A 50 Yard Radius At The Site Where All Objects Were Found To Have Been Fused And Glassified.*"

Did a prehistoric nuclear conflict happen on Planet Earth many aeons ago? The answer to this question is possibly never going to ever be fully verified. However, it does seem likely that the Elites and the Secret Societies are entirely aware of the fact that alien spacecraft appear nearby to every nuclear detonation. This because the detonations can affect the frequencies and vibrations of the geomagnetic leylines on Planet Earth. Does this mean the Elites and the Secret Societies have spent generations wanting to open up dimensional portals to allow malevolent lifeforms to enter the atmosphere of Planet Earth? Such considerations are not likely to be given any scientific confirmation, at least not for many years to come.

CHAPTER 10: SUPERNATURAL REALMS

Most individuals believe the condensed vibrations which seemingly define our existences on Planet Earth, are the only perspective we are able to identify and resonate with. However, the various stories from Germanic Folklore and Irish Folklore are good examples of how many Humans have spent numerous generations interacting with etheric lifeforms, which resonate outside the 3D Holographic Reality of this Material Dimension. From the perspective of Germanic Folklore, these kinds of etheric lifeforms include the Geister (Spirits) or Ghosts, and the Schatten Menschen (Shadow People). Much of Germanic Folklore also mentions the existence of Erscheinungen (Apparitions), and the Seinen (Entities), the Lichtwesen (Light Beings), the Poltergeister (Noisy Spirits), the Gespenster (Specters), Gottesboten (Divine Messengers) and the Teufelen (Devils). Hence, it is not by chance that over 50 percent of Humans, or 1 in 2 individuals on Planet Earth have encountered some sort of paranormal activity, which has connections with these kinds of etheric lifeforms.

The various storylines of Irish Folklore constantly mention the lifeforms which roam across the landscapes of Ireland. Some of these lifeforms include the Aonáin (Entities), and the Daoine Scáth (Shadow People). Over many generations, Irish Folklore became even more enriched, and this meant other etheric lifeforms such as the Taibhsí (Spirits) or Ghosts, Dealramhai (Apparitions), Taibhsí Torann (Noisy Spirits), Spheicoirí (Specters), Beithe Solas (Light Beings), Aingilh (Angels) and Diabhail (Devils), became prevalent in the stories that were told. Before urbanisation became so prevalent, many villages and towns did not have street lights, or domestic electricity supplies. Hence, the nighttimes were seen as very frightening and eery for the residents, and who resided in the villages and towns of Ireland were locations where various kinds of paranormal activity seemingly constantly occurred. Whole communities across Ireland, and Britain and Mainland Europe would become immensely fearful and paranoia if howling and screeching noises were heard in the darkness, especially if the villagers and townsfolk sensed an invisible presence, or if a graveyard was nearby, or there was a Full Moon.

Most individuals see luminosity and darkness as good versus evil, and therefore as exact opposites, even though this is not the case. We are taught that these electromagnetic polarities directly oppose each other, when in actuality such polarities are just different ways of perceiving any situation. In the movies from Hollywood, the directors and producers like to exemplify the light as the Angels, the bringers of hope, who counteract against darkness as the Demons from the Infernal Regions of the Lower Astral.

However, the seemingly apparent polarities of good and evil are subjective concepts which resonate in the 3D Reality of this Material Dimension, but this is not exactly the case when it comes to the vibrations of the Astral Plane. Therefore, dualism is creatively presented and conveyed, in the movies, with engaging storylines, but these are actually fictional representations of what good and evil are truly about.

There are malevolent etheric lifeforms which are designed to spiritually test certain Humans, and these include the perverted and devious Incubus (Reclining Upon Entity), which resides in the Infernal Regions of the Lower Astral, that has a masculine resonant identity.

According to Medieval European Folklore, the Incubus seeks out female Humans that it can have sexual intercourse with. Additionally, the corresponding female version is called a Succubus (Reclining Beneath Entity), which tries to erotically seduce male Humans. Across the countries of Mainland Europe, sexual union with an Incubus was supposed to result in the birth of Hedge Witches, Devils, and hybridised versions of Humans, such as the Cambionum (Replacers) and the Changelings. Both the Incubi and Succubi were known to be Amantium Daemonae (Provider Lovers), and in Medieval European Folklore, any repeated sexual activity with an Incubus or a Succubus would result in the deterioration of the medical and psychiatric health of an individual, which in some circumstances would actually result in their biological death.

The nasty Incubus is a truly horrid lifeform which focuses on the sexual frequencies and vibrations of female Humans, so they can be exploited in the nighttime. Indeed, when these etheric lifeforms collectively act, they become known as the Incubi (Reclining Upon Entities). Additionally, the comparable Succubus, does the opposite and focuses on the sexual frequencies of vulnerable male Humans. Such etheric lifeforms apparently functioned together and would therefore become defined as the Succubi (Reclining Beneath Entities), whilst they secluded unwitting individuals. Many stories have been told in Medieval European Folklore about the Incubi and Succubi who like to consistently visit Humans during the nighttime. In the Holy Bible, it is clearly stated that an etheric lifeform can trick a Human by pretending to be pure and benevolent.

"And No Wonder, For Satan Himself Masquerades As An Angel Of Light".
2 Corinthians 11:14

The choirs of Angels were created as facilitators of the Divine Creation by the Universal Creator. Wherefore, the representation of Lucifer, as the Light Bearer who is also known as Satan or The Adversary, originally indicated how Lucifer had once been the leading Archangel in the Heavenly Kingdom and Celestial Hyperspace. From the perspective of the Greek Orthodox Church the leading Fallen Angel known as Lucifer was called Phōsphoros, as the evil lifeform was seen as one of the Astra Planētoi (Star Wanderers), who specifically existed as some kind of Astrikí Theótita (Astral Deity) and likewise functioned as the Planēta Aphrodítē (Wandering Foamy Being) or the Planet Venus.

Because of the carbon dioxide and sulphur dioxide atmosphere which surrounds the Planet Venus, it became known as the Avgerinós (Morning Star) to the Greek Orthodox Church, as it shimmered with tinges of greenish blue, like the skyline during sunrise in the early hours on the Greek Islands and the Mediterranean Basin. Additionally, certain stories from Greek Folklore mention how the Morning Star is actually defined as Heōsphoros (Dawn Bringer), where the skyline colours sometimes vary from reddish to orangish hues. The carbon dioxide and sulphur dioxide atmosphere which surrounds the Planet Venus does seemingly have connections with Lucifer, as we learn in the Holy Bible, that the Fallen Angel rules over Hell or the location called Sheol (Underworld), where brimstone or sulphur pervades with such prevalence.

When we look at this concept from a religious perspective, the choirs of Angels have always been perceived as transdimensional Divine Spirits and from what has been revealed in the Abrahamic Religions, are the Celestial Envoys of the Universal Creator. The choirs of Angels are said to reside in the Heavenly Kingdom, and observe the affairs of Human Beings on Planet Earth. Why does the religion of Christianity make a connection between the Fallen Angel called Lucifer and stellar masses? Does this indicate that the Fallen Angel had originally descended from the a location in the Milky Way Galaxy, the Sagittarius Dwarf Elliptical Galaxy or from somewhere else in the Physical Universe?

The three Abrahamic Religions often depict Angels as the Celestial Envoys who are there to give Humans specific perspectives about the Universal Creator, as most individuals could never truly comprehend the profound divinity of the Heavenly Kingdom and Celestial Hyperspace, which emanate from the Universal Creator. Some individuals find it easier to use the Abrahamic Religions to connect with the divinity of the Universal Creator. Every resplendent aspect of the Angels is concerned with functioning as protectors and guides for Humans, and they also function as the superluminal facilitators of the Universal Creator, from within any resonant location of the Divine Creation, such as the Astral Worlds and the Physical Universe.

Some of the Angels have specific names, such as Michael, Raphael, Gabriel and Ariel, or titles, such as Seraphim (Fiery Beings) or the Cherubim (Evoking Beings). Within the Abrahamic Religions, there were many Angels that were expelled from the Heavenly Kingdom and Celestial Hyperspace. They became the distorted Angels, who the Fallen Angel known as Lucifer, as the Light Bearer, would rule over. In the Hebrew Language, the concept of a Fallen Angel is defined as Helel, which means Shining Being.

The word 'Daemon' is from the Greek Language and denotes a 'Spirit' or inverted 'Divine Power,' much like the word 'Genius' is from the Latin Language, and is defined as the 'Custodial Spirit' or the 'Moral Spirit' who governs an individual through his or her lifetime. Another definition of the word 'Genius' indicates it refers to a 'Guardian Deity' or a 'Guardian Spirit' which watches over each Human from birth, to monitor their spirituality, incarnations and dormant talents. Within its most basic meaning the word 'Demon' actually means 'Provider.' Now it is interesting to note how this meaning from the Greek Language does not represent something that is evil or exists as malevolent darkness.

During the time of the Early Roman Empire, cult statues of various Numina Sidereum (Astral Deities), that were also called the Deorum Sidereorum (Astral Deities), became very iconic, because this cultural process began to represent the seemingly polarised impulses of good and evil. Over thousands of years religious conditioning became the dominant method of societal manipulation, as it was used to restrict the thinking of the Roman Citizens. During the Paleolithic Age, the Mesolithic Age and the Neolithic Age the communities of primitive Humans would adhere to and constantly follow the advice of the appointed Warlock, or even the Shaman or a Witch, and revered them as kinds of Astral Deities. But when the inverted kinds of religious programming began to dominate societal trends, it could be used to constantly influence the thoughts of the populace.

Additionally, the collective adherence to each aspect that defines Western Occultism and Ceremonial Magic, by the Elites and the Secret Societies of Planet Earth, has been done to ensure they can keep themselves in positions of leadership. The communities of Pagans and Christians in Mainland Europe believed these Astral Deities were the Sanatores Divinum (Divine Healers). But the same Astral Deities may have actually been dimensional tricksters, who were really Demons that had to disguise themselves, so they could deceive the minds of Humans, and cause extensive psychological and emotional disruption.

The famous English Occultist and Ceremonial Magician known as Aleister Crowley, apparently summoned a Demon, during a sexual ritual that he performed as part of the Amalantrah Working in New York City. Additionally, it is well known that Aleister Crowley summoned Demons next to Loch Ness, which is southwest of Inverness, in the Scottish Highlands of Northern Scotland. With tremendous fascination, Aleister Crowley used aspects of Ceremonial Magic at Boleskine House, which is located nearby to Loch Ness, in the Scottish Highlands, to summon Demons from the Infernal Regions of the Lower Astral. This summoning occurred between the 17 February 1899 and the 26 October 1913. Once the Demons had transitioned into actuality, Boleskine House became very haunted, because Aleister Crowley had opened dimensional portals with his Ceremonial Magic. The summoned Demons would make loud, disturbing noises, move furniture about and roll up carpets. During the nighttime, certain Demons would attack any occupants who stayed in the property.

The highly etheric Ghost is the Astral Spirit of a deceased Human, or bird or mammal, that seems to be animated. Sometimes a Ghost is called a Spook. Because of the numerous stories which have been gathered about Ghosts, it has become clear that such etheric lifeforms widely vary in appearance, from existing as some kind of invisible presence to displaying a translucent or barely visible wispy shape, whilst others look similar to a corporeal lifeform. Whenever a deliberate attempt to contact the Spirit of a deceased person is carried out, this is called Necromancy. Sometimes, individuals use Spiritism to contact a deceased relative or friend, as this is called 'Séance', which is a French Language word for 'Seated.' Other terms associated with a Ghost include the words Haunt and Phantom. There are specific traits which these kinds of Astral Spirits continually exhibit, and some of these mean it could be a Grey Lady, a Spectral Lady, a Brown Lady or a Headless Ghost.

The Bell Witch Haunting apparently began on the 29 October 1817, when John William Bell Senior reported observing telekinetic movement, and banging sounds at his residency within the city of Adams, which is located in Robertson County. Numerous other hauntings were also reported at the time across Northern Tennessee, in that area of the Southern United States. The case was made famous by the reports of General Andrew Jackson, who later became the Seventh U.S. President. The daughter of John William Bell Senior, who was called Betsy Bell, was of certain interest to the Bell Witch Haunting, as she was physically attacked by the etheric lifeform.

There are many areas of Culver City in Southern California, which are known to be haunted, and the Holy

Cross Catholic Cemetery is a good example of this. Just like with this building, a specific house on Braddock Drive in Los Angeles County became renowned after the movie called The Entity, was produced and broadcast. The Entity was directed by Sidney Joseph Furie in 1982, and is based on a true story about Doris Bither, who was a single mother that was trying to raise four children. Doris Bither had moved from Santa Monica during the 5 August 1974, into a dilapidated house in Braddock Drive, in Culver City, within Los Angeles County, Southern California.

Once a few weeks had passed, Doris Bither started to be physically and sexually abused by the Entity from the Infernal Regions of the Lower Astral. Because she was frightened and desperate to find a solution, Doris Bither agreed to participate in an elaborate scientific experiment which Doctor Barry Taff and Kerry Gaynor had methodically developed. This involved them constructing a full mock-up of her home at Braddock Drive, in Culver City, which they built at the University of California, Los Angeles (UCLA). With logical intent, Doctor Barry Taff and Kerry Gaynor wanted to lure the Entity from the Astral World into a trap by freezing the etheric lifeform with liquid helium. Many of you will probably think that such an idea sounds utterly crazy, but this experiment did actually happen.

The investigation began on the 22 August 1974, in Culver City, which like so many other areas in Southern California, has numerous convergent ley lines. Even though Doctor Barry Taff and Kerry Gaynor had a lot of scientific knowledge about paranormal activity, the presence of the Entity would become an intensely bizarre interaction. Believing that this would be an open and shut case Doctor Barry Taff and Kerry Gaynor showed up at the house of Doris Bither. Because they did not expect much to happen, Doctor Barry Taff and Kerry Gaynor, had no idea the case would become one of the biggest cases in the annals of paranormal history.

Doctor Barry Taff and his research associate Kerry Gaynor were overheard talking about the paranormal by a woman in a local bookstore on the 16 August 1974. The woman approached the two men, and one of them, who was called Kerry Gaynor, talked with her. She mentioned to him that her house was haunted. She gave some details about the haunting and Kerry Gaynor told her that he would discuss this with his associate. After the meeting in the bookstore, Doctor Barry Taff and Kerry Gaynor arrived at the Braddock Drive, in Culver City home on the 22 August 1974. Doris Bither, a petite woman of 34 greeted them. Doris Bither lived in the small home with her 6 year old daughter and her three sons. Her daughter was 6 years old, and her boys were 10, 13 and 16.

With a certain urgency, Doris Bither told Doctor Barry Taff and Kerry Gaynor that when she moved into the property at Braddock Drive on the 5 August 1974, an elderly female Mexican Curandera knocked at her door and warned Doris that the house was evil and then stated *"You Need To Get Out! I Used To Live Here In This Old House, Back When It Was Just A Farm And I Was A Little Girl. There Is Something Very Evil Here. This Place Is Haunted And You Need To Get Out!"*

Brian, who is the son of Doris Bither, said that his mother started experimenting with a Ouija Board or Talking Board. She actually held meetings with friends during 1962, so that each of them could talk with Astral Spirits, and continued to do so until 1969. Doris Bither then started to mix this paranormal activity with cocaine and alcohol. She had also struggled with psychiatric and mental health issues since her childhood. Because Doris Bither had experienced a very abusive upbringing, she carried a lot of emotional stress and trauma. Additionally, she was a single mother of four kids, and therefore Doris Bither may have been also searching for answers from the Spirit World, and her motivation to do this caused a vibrational shift which opened a dimensional portal into the Infernal Regions of the Lower Astral.

The use of the Ouija Board by Doris Bither may have opened some kind of dimensional portal, but the Entity may have already been there, just as the female Mexican Curandera had described. When she moved from the property, the attacks from the Entity against Doris Bither immediately stopped and no reports of the Entity were ever made again. Hence, was the property situated on some kind of inverted ley line convergence? The case of Doris Bither and the Entity, seemingly had similarities with the disruption that Poltergeists sometimes cause. However, the Entity which Doris Bither encountered was far more sinister, and had traits which indicated the lifeform was comparable to a Demon because of its behaviour.

The word 'Poltergeist' originates from the German Language, and means 'Noisy Spirit'. Most descriptions of Poltergeists show they have the capability to pinch, bite, hit and trip Humans. As so many individuals have mentioned similar behaviour patterns for this kind of etheric lifeform, it is therefore clear that Poltergeists are capable of moving or levitating objects, such as furniture and cutlery, or can make sometimes bang on doors, floors and ceilings.

Another kind of Astral Spirit, are the Orbs which are arguably one of the most common etheric lifeforms. They are often sighted when ley lines converge or other kinds of paranormal activity have become prevalent. Many of the Orbs have been photographed. The unseen Funnel Spirits apparently exist in the chilly rooms of houses, where they create an unsettling feeling which most residents intensely feel. Apparently the various Funnel Spirits are said to be the etheric residue of loved ones or previous homeowners who have come back to visit their former occupancies.

Other etheric lifeforms such as the Shadow People are known to exist in the Infernal Regions of the Lower Astral. Have you ever awoken in the middle of the night to see a darkened mass somewhere in your bedroom or lounge? If you have observed such an etheric lifeform, the darkened mass could well be a red eyed Shadow Person. Hence, the Astral Spirits called the Shadow People are described as having the shape of a figure or some kind of amorphic mass. Sometimes the Shadow People display glowing red eyes, and they are often shaped like a Humanoid, but never seem to have any facial features.

Over certain generations the Apparitions, that are Wraiths, who were once Human Beings, can sometimes appear as portents of an imminent death, and therefore reveals that individual will soon become deceased, and their Soul Personality will leave behind the condensed vibrations of Planet Earth and enter into the 4D Holographic Reality of the Astral Plane.

Among the gnarled trees and shrubs of Highgate Wood and Queens Wood, in Highgate, North London, are ley lines which converge and various Astral Spirits have been observed by residents in these Wood. Additionally, it is known that Coldfall Wood and Bluebell Wood, in Muswell Hill, are somewhat haunted. Before the Roman Legions invaded and then occupied Celtic Britain, the landmass was entirely inhabited by Celtic Britons and the Druids. They used the ley lines as part of their worship and the location of Highgate Woods was also used as a burial ground during the Bubonic Plague, which lasted from the 24 June 1348 to the 7 December 1349, in the United Kingdom. From knowing this, it becomes clear that districts of London have become very paranormal locations.

Even though most individuals never seem to realise how important Spirits, Entities, Angels, and Demons really are, such lifeforms perform the vibratory function of making the experiencer become more aware of themselves. When this kind of supernatural interaction occurs, the experiencer is actually perceiving the event from just beyond the spacetime parameters of this Physical Universe. Are etheric tricksters really pulling certain Human Beings into the darker frequencies, in which they can manipulate the Human Psyche? Maybe that is not what is happening, and instead such existences are part of the learning which different Humans require as part of their own incarnations on Planet Earth. We must remember that malevolent etheric lifeforms can only attach to the lower vibrations which emit from an individual who suffers from depression and substance addiction issues, or who carries specific traumas from their childhood or adolescent years. However, if an individual can resolve their own psychological and emotional problems, their own vibrations will then shift, and therefore neither can then correlate as they have created the boundary. That is why healing trauma is so important for our growth.

Numerous urban and rural communities around Planet Earth continually focus on the lower frequencies which are always there. For most, the usage of alcohol, drugs, pornography, the commercial misinformation of the television stations, and online streaming platforms have become integral parts of their private lifestyles. Most individuals do not realise they are following inverted forms of predictive programming which have been developed by the Elites and their Secret Societies. They have to imprint digital and electromagnetic distortions into the minds of Humans as the spell which is covertly intended to manipulate the thoughts of the observer.

Various kinds of paranormal phenomena most certainly exist, but we have a much higher vibration that we can attune to, in which we use a brighter and more expansive kind of Human Consciousness. We have chosen to incarnate on Planet Earth where there are a multitude of interlinked frequencies and vibrations, and this means the 3D Holographic Reality of this Material Dimension does seem very tangible, because everything has become so condensed here, even though many frequencies resonate beyond the slowed vibrations that define physicality.

CHAPTER 11: BRITISH CRYPTIDS

The incredible landscapes of Celtic Britain have been used for thousands of years to establish territories of martial dominance, and conflict have arisen. However, none of this compares to the stories about the unusual Cryptids which seemingly exist within the British Isles. Although different kinds of Cryptids exist in many locations on Planet Earth, it is this landmass which is rather special, as so many stories have been told about the Cryptids which frequently reside in the United Kingdom.

Within the geographic reaches of the United Kingdom are numerous kinds of etheric lifeforms which include the Owlman, the various Mountain Giants, the unusual Astral Entity called Spring Heeled Jack and the highly elusive Woodwose (Forest Beings), that also became revered in English Folklore, when they were given similar descriptive names such as the Wodewose (Forest Beings), and the Wudwas (Forest Beings). Further cultural divergences occurred in villages and towns acros England, and resulted in the Cryptids becoming defined as the Wudewas (Forest Beings), and the Wuduwāsa (Forest Beings) or the Wudewāsa (Forest Beings). These specific etheric lifeforms have been described in the chivalric story from Welsh Folklore called Sir Gawain And The Green Knight, that was written by John Massey.

Across the Scottish Highlands of Northern Scotland many kinds of Great Serpents were known to have resided in Loch Morar, and on many occasions were seen in other aquatic environments which include Loch Lochy, Loch Arkaig, Loch Oich, Loch Linnhe, Loch Quoich and Loch Shiel. Other aquatic creatures such as the Nwyvre (Water Dragon) of the River Taff at Cardiff, in Southern Wales, became legendary presences for the local Celtic Britons. Some of these stories are unexplainable and leaves you wondering what kind of concealed etheric lifeforms exist in the landscapes of Celtic Britain or even beneath the landmass itself, within the locations which have become defined as the Ceudyllau Disgleirio (Shining Caverns) of the Daear Bant (Hollow Earth).

One of the most horrific creatures is the Beste Hwithranow (Questing Beast), which also became similarly defined as the Beste Glatisant (Questing Beast), which is a noisy mutant which the physique of a Reptile and a Mammal. This bizarre etheric lifeform was initially seen on the 28 September 1346. There were other kinds of lifeforms that were known to be present throughout Cornwall, in South West England, and these included the Euthviles Gonyow (Moorland Monsters). Such kinds of Cryptids were similarly known as Tebelvestes Gonyow (Moorland Monsters), and the Spyrysyon Gwedhek (Woodland Spirits), and the Spyryjyon Gwedhek (Woodland Spirits). Apparently, these creatures frequently roamed across Cornwall, but the Questing Beast was the most physically repulsive looking of them all. From those who observed the Questing Beast, it appeared to have the head of a snake, the body of a leopard, the legs of a stag, the thighs and tail of a lion. The bizarre looking Questing Beast was believed to have existed next to the River Camel, near Bodmin Moor, in North Eastern Cornwall and midst other nearby areas in South West England. In Volume 1, Book 1, Chapter 19 of the prose called Le Morte D'Arthur, that was published on the 23 February 1485, the following was written about this British Cryptid, by the English Novelist, Sir Thomas Mallory:

"*This Beast Went To The Well And Drank, And The Noise Was In The Beast's Belly Like Unto The Questing Of Thirty Couple Hounds, But All The While The Beast Drank There Was No Noise In The Beast's Belly.*"

Along with this, are the numerous stories about the Beast of Bodmin Moor which is a massive Phantom Feline, which has brown fur and glowing red eyes. The Beast of Bodmin Moor inhabits the granite uplands of North Eastern Cornwall. But close to that area you also have the Beast of Dartmoor, which roams the uplands across Dartmoor National Park, in South Devon and elsewhere in South Western England. The Beast of Dartmoor is described as some kind of large furry wild boar or swine, that has glowing red eyes.

With this, are other types of Phantom Cats, which are also called British Large Cats or Alien Big Cats, that seem to appear from nowhere and then start to roam about the rural locations of the United Kingdom. The Beast of Cumbria Is reported to be a dark looking Wildcat that appears to be a Panther, which has been seem roaming near to the village of Penrith, in the Eden District of East Cumbria. Additionally, the United Kingdom is a landmass where many other Phantom Felines prevalently exist, and these include the Hull Hell Cat which has been observed in the village of North Cave, in the East Riding of Yorkshire, the Bury Beast, which is a dark Panther that residents have observed in the market town of Bury, that is located next to the River Irwell, in Greater Manchester.

Numerous sightings of Phantom Felines have occurred elsewhere, such as with the Wildcat of Wakefield, which is a dark looking Panther, which apparently roams the meadows around the city of Wakefield, on the River Calder, in West Yorkshire. With this, other sightings like the Bedfordshire Big Cat or Beast of Silsoe, which is a Panther which regularly forages nearby the village of Silsoe in Central Bedfordshire.

Are these Phantom Felines using the ley lines of the United Kingdom, to explore the countryside? Where do these Phantom Felines actually come from? Because none of these creatures have ever been caught, does this mean they are etheric? There seems to be so many sightings of Phantom Felines, and credible photographic evidence does confirm these kinds of Mammals are obviously real. Here are some more details about sightings of Phantom Felines that have occurred in the United Kingdom. Firstly, there is the Pershore Panther, which is apparently some kind of dark coloured Puma that has been observed around the market town of Pershore in the Wychavon District of Worcestershire. Further similar etheric lifeforms have been seen, and these are the Beast of Bucks, which is a Puma which likes to explore Tom Burts Hill, in the market town of High Wycombe in Buckinghamshire and the Wildcat of Warwickshire, that is a pale brownish Lynx, that has been seen nearby the village of Great Alne in Warwickshire.

Alongside these are the Beast of Broomfield, which is a huge Wildcat that likes to roam nearby the village and suburb of Broomfield, next to Chelmsford, in Essex, and the Dartmoor Lynx, which constantly roams across Dartmoor National Park in South Devon. There are many ley line convergences that resonate in the United Kingdom, and therefore do the Phantom Felines have frequencies that means they are not exactly existing in a bodily form.

Other similar etheric lifeforms such as the Beast of Cornwall, that is a lion, which has been seen along the River Lynher, near the village of Saint Germans in East Cornwall, and the Dartmoor Devil, which is said to be a leopard that likes to forage in Dartmoor National Park, in South Devon. The unusual Suffolk Panther has been seen in the market town of Thetford, in the Breckland District of South Norfolk, and the market town of Homersfield and South Elmham Saint Mary, on the banks of the River Waveney in North Suffolk.

Because these creatures are constantly described as Panthers or Jaguars, it means these kinds of Mammals have habitat and ecosystem connections with Central America and South America. This is also the situation with those Phantom Felines that have been described as Pumas or Cougars, which means they might have connections with different locations in North America and South America.
Over 250 years ago, the renowned British Politician known as William Cobbett became the first individual to encounter the Alien Big Cat, as he recalled in his book, Rural Rides, where on the 28 April 1763, he observed a Phantom Feline that was silently climbing into a carved out elm tree in the grounds of Waverley Abbey. This location is nearby to Farnham, which is a market town where paranormal activity has become a regular occurrence. Other areas of Waverley Borough in West Surrey have also become locations where the Phantom Felines are seen. According to the story, William Cobbett had observed the Phantom Feline on the during the 28 April 1763, so maybe these kinds of etheric lifeforms have inhabited parts of the United Kingdom for a very long time. Perhaps the different tree species emit frequencies and vibrations that somehow correlate with

the Phantom Felines and the Astral World. Maybe this is why the Irish Druids and the British Druids had such a fascination with trees.

The incredibly elusive Cryptid known as the Mawnan Owlman and the Cowanden, has been known to have revealed its presence in the villages of Mawnan and Helford Passage, and with them, certains hamlets such as Carlidnack, Bareppa, Penwarne and Durgan, in South Cornwall. Many individuals have observed the Mawnan Owlman flying over the cove of Maenporth, and other nearby areas in South West England. The etheric Mawnan Owlman appears to be some kind of feathery Humanoid that has the head of a Owl and winged arms. The etheric lifeform was first sighted in the village of Mawnan, in South Cornwall.

A large Owlman was seen hovering above the tower of Saint Mawnan and Saint Stephen's Church, in the village of Mawnan on the 17 April 1976, by two sisters called June Melling and Vicky Melling. Another unusual Owlman, that is known as the Ulemann, and is likewise called the Üllemann, was observed by numerous residents in the village of Alfriston, in the Wealden District of East Sussex, during the 17 October 2013 and the 16 March 2014. For many individuals who resided in East Sussex during the Medieval Period, this kind of Cryptid was defined as the Houtemann and the Hutemann.

According to the story, two close friends called Sally Chapman and Barbara Perry, who were both aged 14 at the time, were camping next to Saint Mawnan and Saint Stephen's Church, on the 23 August 1976, when they were confronted by the Owlman, who had a large bipedal physique, and pointed ears, glowing eyes, and pincer-like claws. Sally Chapman and Barbara Perry ran away. Both of them later drew what they had observed. The description of the Owlman is somewhat comparable to the physique of the Mothman. However, the Owlman has never been known to cause mayhem as the Mothman did in the city of Point Pleasant in Mason County. Across much of West Virginia, as with other areas in the South Eastern United States, a lot of paranormal activity seems to be the normality.

Throughout multiple locations in the Scottish Highlands, the Inner Hebrides and the Outer Hebrides, are places where prehistoric Cryptids and paranormal activities have become prevalent. For many individuals, the Scottish Highlands are most famous for the Loch Ness Monster. However, there are numerous other Cryptids that frequent the rural areas of Scotland. For example, there is the Fear Liath Mhòr, which is also known as the Big Gray Man. This etheric life form is said to inhabit the summit of Ben Macdui or Beinn MacDuibh, upon the Cairngorm Mountains in North Eastern Scotland. Supposedly you can hear its disembodied footsteps in the gravel on Ben Macdui and when the fog thins, a very large Hairy Humanoid becomes observable. The Big Gray Man has been sighted many times and perhaps the refractions of photons in the misty weather, actually create the outline of this Cryptid.

The countryside of Northern Scotland has long been used as rural habitats by the Cryptids which are still observed even to this day. For example, there is the Each Uisge (Water Horse), which is an etheric life form that relishes the consumption of meat. This kind of Water Horse apparently exists midst Loch Shiel, in the Lochaber District of the Scottish Highlands.

Every one of the Water Horses were said to be shape changers, similar to what is called the Cailpeach (Young Horse) or Kelpie. Which took on the physique of either a glistening aquatic equine, a handsome man or beautiful women. The elusive Uisge would usually approach a Scottish Celt as a seemingly friendly horse, which beckoned them to mount it, and when they did, the Uisge would then drag them into Loch Ness.

Both Scotland and Ireland are landmasses which are where the legendary Beithigh Uisce (Water Beasts), such as the Mòrag (Great Being), and the Nathair Uaine (Green Serpent), and the Maighdean Locha (Lake Maiden), have become integral aspects of Celtic Folklore. Other kinds of aquatic creatures also became prevalent in the stories of Celtic Folklore, and these were the Snámhóir Adharcach (Horned Swimmer), the Mhuc Sheilche (Turtle Swine), and of course the Loch Ness Monster.

The bizarre Loch Ness Monster, which many know as Nessie, is some kind of aquatic Reptile, that is quite possibly a species of Plesiosaur. Indeed, this etheric life form has been mentioned in Scottish Folklore for many generations, and is said to inhabit Loch Ness in the Scottish Highlands of Northern Scotland. It is often described as having a massive, long neck, with one or more humps protruding from it, whenever the creature emerges.

Whether or not the Loch Ness Monster is a Plesiosaur has never been verified, and this kind of aquatic Reptile was brought to worldwide attention when Aldie Mackay observed the Loch Ness Monster on the 16 January 1933. Evidence of its existence is anecdotal, with a number of disputed photographs and sonar readings.

The first recorded sighting of Loch Ness Monster was by the Irish Christian Abbot called Saint Columba Mhac Conaill, on the 21 October 565 AD and there have been sightings ever since. An interesting point to Loch Ness it is the second deepest watery depression and contains more freshwater than all the streams and lakes combined in the England and Wales, so it would be very easy for something to conceal itself in these murky waters.

The famous British Gynaecologist called Robert Kenneth Wilson, had travelled from London to Scotland for a holiday, and whilst there he photographed the Loch Ness Monster on the 28 March 1934. Everything about the photograph is wrong, because the scale of the Loch Ness Monster is too small and the ripples of the waves are too large. So this photograph is definitely fake. However, the reason why the main stream tabloid newspapers in the United Kingdom of Great Britain, such as the Daily Express and the Evening Standard, so widely reported on the fake sighting of the Loch Ness Monster, was because it could then be used to ridicule the entire subject over the long term and if any real photographs were ever taken, most individuals would believe they were also part of a hoax.

Others did eventually photograph the Loch Ness Monster, and the British Cryptozoologist known as Timothy Kay Dinsdale, was such an individual. He managed to photograph the Loch Ness Monster on the 23 April 1960. The photograph Timothy Kay Dinsdale took is believed to be real, and was used in Volume 15 of The Unexplained: Mysteries of Mind, Space, and Time, which was a partwork magazine that was produced by Orbis Publishing in the United Kingdom, from 1980 to 1983.

Surprisingly there have also been alleged sightings of the Sasquatch or Bigfoot in the Caerphilly Woodlands, the Brecon Beacons National Park and the Caerphilly Mountain, near to Cardiff, in Southern Wales, and in Rendlesham Forest, which is located in a part of East Suffolk where many ley lines converge. As with the Sasquatch or Bigfoot sightings of North America, the bipedal etheric lifeforms which are seen in Wales and England seem to have the features of a Simian, or a Ursid, or a Canine. Do these Humanoids psychically use the ley lines and subterranean passageways which course beneath the United Kingdom?

During the 22 November 2012, some kind of Bigfoot was reported in the newspapers called The Sun and the Daily Mail. Apparently the residents of Tunbridge Wells in West Kent had been terrorised by an 8 foot tall Hairy Humanoid that had fiery red eyes. Although no physical evidence of this has ever been found, many residents in Tunbridge Wells observed the bipedal etheric life form. Because the Bigfoot was seen by so many individuals, it was eventually called the Kentish Apeman and the British Bigfoot.

With these kinds of Cryptids is the Pinneoten (Pencil Giant) of Northumberland, Cumbria, Westmorland and County Durham, in Northern England, who was another version of the Woodland Wild Man, which is an etheric lifeform that is seen in the Yellowham Wood of West Dorset and the Duncliffe Wood of North Dorset. Hence, the list of these Crytpids is endless and does show that beyond this reality, numerous etheric lifeforms prevalently exist.

So where do these Cryptids actually reside? Do some of the Cryptids inhabit the countryside of the United Kingdom? From what has been mentioned about these kinds of Cryptids, it does seem that some of them inhabit the 4D Holographic Reality of the Astral Plane, and have the ability to psychically transition into visibility on Planet Earth for certain temporal durations. There have been many occasions when Unidentified Aerial Phenomena (UAP) seem to appear whilst Cryptids are present in a rural location. Additionally, the areas where alien spacecraft transition into visibility are where geomagnetic ley lines resonate and converge.

Did malevolent Ultraterrestrials or Extraterrestrials deliberately alter the genetics of Humans, to prevent us from easily tuning into the varied frequencies and vibrations which resonate from the Physical Universe or the 4D Holographic Reality of the Astral Plane? Are we incarnations on Planet Earth that have therefore become to condensed to instantly move our thoughts and cognition into other electromagnetic locations beyond spacetime? Maybe the ancestors of the Elites and their Secret Societies were covertly tasked with the deliberate suppression of our vibrational connection with the other subspace expanses, and did so because they did not want Humans to develop any psychical or telepathic links with certain benevolent Ultraterrestrials and Extraterrestrials.

The electromagnetic resonances which define this 3D Holographic Reality of this Material Dimension, have many dimensional levels, and we collectively exist in one of them. However, there are individuals who have the ability to sometimes perceive the Astral Worlds. Because we are conditioned to only believe that existing on Planet Earth is the only truth, most individuals never perceive the subspace realities that are around them. Again, we have to consider whether or not the genetics of Humans been intentionally manipulated and disconnected. Although it makes logical sense to always questions the validity of the British Cryptids, they are not just products of the imagination or the fantasies of Humans. Therefore, we must always remain open to the possibility which these interactions can bring.

CHAPTER 12: ARTIFICIAL INTELLIGENCE

Some individuals think that Artificial Intelligence or AI is a scientific process which only began on the 9 October 1986, when the cognitive psychologist and computer scientist called Geoffrey Everest Hinton and the cognitive psychologist known as David Everett Rumelhart, published a research paper on artificial neural networks in Volume 323 Issue 6088 of the weekly scientific journal called Nature. However, when we look at prehistoric statues, artifacts, relics, drawings and paintings there are so many different references to Artificial Intelligence and other kinds of advanced Occult Technology.

Along with this, whenever any prehistoric statues, artifacts, relics, drawings and paintings are found, some have imprints or etchings of a spacecraft, which is now defined as some kind of Unidentified Aerial Phenomena (UAP). Maybe these prehistoric remnants were versions of Artificial Intelligence that could operate and interact with us in ways that even the computer programmers of Silicon Valley, in Northern California, would not be able to comprehend.

Although computing machines have become the defining parameter of Artificial Intelligence, thousands of years ago in countries such as Classical Greece and Dynastic China, there were various kinds of mechanistic engines which defined Artificial Intelligence during that specific time, and they were devices which had been designed to function in collaboration with the cognition of Humans. For example, in the book series called '*The 9 Divine Worlds Of Primordial Mathematics,*' which the author known as Luis Daniel Maldonado Fonken, profoundly wrote, are explanatory calculations that use the guidelines of prehistoric arithmetic. Such calculations eventually became versions of the mechanistic engine and therefore started to function as essential cultural aspects of Humans. Because this integration occurred, it exemplified the subjects of individual and collective awareness, the spectrum of emotions and behaviour patterns which many Humans often experience.

More than 2,500 years ago, many stories arose from Greek Mythology, Roman Mythology, Indian Mythology and Chinese Mythology which describe artificial life, self-moving devices, automata and the enhancements of Humans, and how these visions relate to and reflect the ancient invention of real animated machines. The first robot to walk the Planet Earth was known as Tálōs (Shining Being). Over the aeons, such a mechanical lifeform also became known as Tálus (Shining Being), and similarly as Tálōn (Shining Being), who was a Chálkinos Gígantas, Χάλκινος Γίγαντας (Bronze Giant) that became defined as Talos, who stood 98 feet or 30 metres in height. He was crafted by the notable Greek Deity called Hephaestus Olimbos. For many Classical Greeks, the massive looking Tálōs, Tálus or Tálōn was defined as the Metallikó Fýlaka, Μεταλλικό Φύλακα (Quarry Guardian), who was likewise named the Metallikó Kidemóna, Μεταλλικό Κηδεμόνα (Quarry Guardian), because he radiantly gleamed and shimmered on the Greek Island of Crete.

There has been numerous amounts of research and projects created around Artificial Intelligence that have been given no public disclosure or later presented to us as be somekind of conspiracy theory. But the Philadelphia Experiment which happened on the 28 October 1943, became another of the contributory programs which the Elites and their Secret Societies covertly use. The same reasoning was used to ensure the Greada Treaty could occur during the 20 February 1954, and the development of Project MK-Ultra from the 13 April 1953 and onward until the 18 November 1953. These planned and scheduled programs allowed for covert scientific research to be used, and therefore such events can be defined as part of a conspiracy, but they are certainly not part of any theory.

Was it an accident that an exponential development of electronic devices occurred after the Greada Treaty was signed on the 20 February 1954 between U.S. President David Dwight Eisenhower and the Rigelian Grays and the Orion Grays? Was some kind of Occult Technology exchanged and was there a Deep Underground Military Base (DUMB) or a D1 Base constructed directly below Muroc Army Airfield, which eventually became known as Edwards Air Force Base? Were advanced versions of Artificial Intelligence produced after the Greaty Treaty was signed? Does the black goo from the Zeta Reticulan Type A Grays and Zeta Reticulan Type B Grays, have any connection with the Greada Treaty? Did the Rigelian Grays given the United States Army Air Forces (USAAF) some kind of Artificial Intelligence (AI) that was then covertly manufactured?

The science fiction writer from the United Kingdom, known as Sir Arthur Charles Clarke, wrote and then published the epic science fiction story 2001 A Space Odyssey, during the 1 July 1968, which later turned into a film by Stanley Kubrick, with the same name on the 2 April 1968. An interesting note with Arthur C. Clarke in his 1951 book, The Exploration of Space, was used by the aerospace engineer and rocket pioneer from National Socialist Germany, Wernher Magnus

Maximilian Freiherr von Braun, who became commonly known as Wernher von Braun, to convince U.S. President John Franklin Kennedy that it was possible to go to the Moon. Hence, a science fiction book helped to convince the U.S. President John Franklin Kennedy to embark on a space mission. Did Arthur C. Clarke have an insight into this Occult Technology with his science fiction novels? Did Arthur C. Clarke have access to concealed information? Was the 33rd Degree Scottish Rite Freemason, Arthur C. Clarke somehow connected with the Secret Societies that gave him the information so he could publish it within his science fiction novels?

According to the Elites and their Secret Societies, by the 31 December 2035 the collective minds of Humans will be able to communicate with each other as fully unified individuals within the bio digital convergence. The inventor and futurist called Raymond Kurzweil has written books about the subject, and include *The Age of Intelligent Machines* (1990), and The 10 Percent Solution For A Healthy Life (1993). He also wrote other notable books like *The Age Of Spiritual Machines* (1999), *Fantastic Voyage: Live Long Enough To Live Forever* (2004), *The Singularity Is Near* (2005), *Transcend: Nine Steps To Living Well Forever* (2009) and *How To Create A Mind* (2012). Additionally, Raymond Kurzweil is fascinated with transhumanism, the advancement of the scientific and technological singularity and World Futurism. Many believe that by the 31 December 2045, the singularity will have been accomplished because of Artificial Intelligence.

The devout American Christian and paramedic known as Anthony Patch, has mentioned on numerous occasions that the Holy Bible warns of the Mark of the Beast, which is described in *The Book Of Revelation*.

Such writings are likewise called *The Apocalypse of John*. The Mark of the Beast is essentially a part of the digital grid the Elites and their Secret Societies want to create with Artificial Intelligence, which is ultimately concerned with enslaving the minds of Humans and tracking each transaction in a cashless biometric World Community. Much of the research that Anthony Patch has done, reveals how these versions of Artificial Intelligence will be used to further enhance the cybernetic analysis of synthetic lifeforms, the implementation of recorded and condensed digital imagery and the summoning and enshrinement of Demons within computer databases. Hence, the nefarious plans of the Elites and their Secret Societies are intended to delude Humans so their individual thoughts and beliefs can be consistently manipulated. This kind of Artificial Intelligence programming will eventually include the usage of teleportation for the purposes of transporting data as qubits or quantum bits that can be stored away from spacetime.

Any mention of teleportation has to include the Philadelphia Experiment, which happened on the 28 October 1943 when the U.S. Navy attempted to create an electromagnetically charged invisibility cloak for the U.S.S. Eldridge (DE-173), that was a destroyer escort of the Cannon Class. The vessel was apparently teleported 650 KM away from where it was stationed at the Philadelphia Naval Shipyard, in the city of Philadelphia and then appeared in the Norfolk Naval Shipyard, which is located in the city of Portsmouth. Midst the city of Philadelphia, and elsewhere in Pennsylvania, as with the North Eastern United States, are many ley line convergences. Additionally, the same kind of ley line convergences are present in the city of Portsmouth and other areas in Virginia and the Eastern

United States. According to what is known about The Philadelphia Experiment, the former United States Merchant Marine known as Carl Meredith Allen, apparently witnessed the teleportation of the destroyer escort U.S.S. Eldridge. However, there is no way of confirming whether he did or not.

There have always been rumours that link the Philadephia Experiment with the exclusive Serbian inventor Nikola Tesla, who came from the village of Smiljanin, in the Western Lika Region of Croatia. From what has been mentioned, it appears that Nikola Tesla supposedly made the necessary calculations and equations for the Office of Naval Intelligence, and provided his own electromagnetic generators that were used to carry out the teleportation of the U.S.S. Eldridge. Most individuals know that the Unified Field Theory (UFT) of the theoretical physicist Albert Einstein, was used as the basis for the covert teleportation of the U.S.S. Eldridge. Was some kind of Artificial Intelligence used during The Philadelphia Experiment? Different aspects of the advanced Occult Technology that was implemented to carry out the teleportation of the U.S.S. Eldridge, functioned with similar frequencies to those which are emitted from infrastructure servers that use Artificial Intelligence. Would the Office of Naval Intelligence and the U.S. Navy really disclose what occurred during The Philadelphia Experiment? Because such advanced Occult Technology was used to ensure the process of teleportation could be successfully carried out, would the Office of Naval Intelligence and the U.S. Navy allow what happened on the 28 October 1943 to become publicly known?

Even though academics have never confirmed whether or not the Military Industrial Complex (MIC) have managed to accomplish the process of teleportation, what is known is that quantum teleportation does exist. This remote data transference process can be used to send quantum information from an individual at one location to a receiver some distance away. Whether or not the U.S.S. Eldridge was teleported between the Philadelphia Naval Shipyard and Norfolk Naval Shipyard, is certainly questionable. However, quantum teleportation is a real scientific process which involves the sequenced transfer of digital information. Are there connections between the scientific process of quantum and corporeal teleportation which the Military Industrial Complex is furtively involved with developing? Have any of the scientific results from such endeavours been covertly integrated within the academic programs of Artificial Intelligence that are taught and facilitated at Oxford University, Cambridge University, Stanford University and Harvard University? We have to remember that the famous inventor known as Nikola Tesla, once said:

"My Brain Is Only A Receiver, In The Universe There Is A Core From Which 'We' Obtain Knowledge, Strength And Inspiration. I Have Not Penetrated Into The Secrets Of This Core, But I Know It Exists."

Other kinds of Artificial Intelligence were produced during the Neolithic Age. Such developments became further crafted in the Bronze Age, which can be seen with the manufacturing of the Pārada Cakrākāra Yantra (Quicksilver Vortex Engine) during 21 June 4,538 BC. This incredible propulsion device was invented by the Hindu Deities known as Brahma Ishvara, Vishnu Ishvara, Shiva Ishvara, and Raman Ishvara, who was likewise called Ramar Ishvara. Much of the Neolithic Age became a time when numerous kinds of shimmering Vimānaḥ (Traversers) or Vimanas flew across the skies of Vedic India. Each of these Quicksilver Vortex Engines generated anti-gravity and caused electric propulsion to also occur. According to the document called the Vaimānika Śāstra (Traverser Study Manual), the propulsion mechanisms of the Vimanas were based on anti-gravitational Occult Technology, and could resonate with the frequencies of Humans. Because of eventual linguistic variation, the aircraft texts also became known as the Vimānika Śāstra (Traverser Study Manual). Over subsequent generations the document was also defined as the Vymānika Śāstra (Traverser Study Manual) and the Vyamānika Śāstra (Traverser Study Manual). The scientific knowledge of the Vimānaḥ (Traversers), was revealed in the aircraft texts, revealed from the 16 April 1952 to the 13 October 1952 by Gomatham Rituparan Ravikanta Josyer, the texts contain 3,000 Ślokaḥ (Verses) in 8 chapters which Subbaraya Dhruvah Shastry claimed was psychically delivered to him by the Maharishi and Vedic Sage called Bharadvaja Barhaspatya.

During the 14 October 1952 the existence of the text was revealed by Gomatham Ravikanta Josyer, who was also known as G. R. Josyer. He asserted that the Vaimānika Śāstra was written by the Paṇḍita (Wisdom Collector) called Subbaraya Dhruvah Shastry. Gomatham Ravikanta Josyer or G. R. Josyer, had been the Director of the International Academy of Sanskrit Research, in the city of Mysore, when the Vaimānika Śāstra was made publicly available. The population of Hindu Indians in that city and elsewhere across the Karnataka State of Southern India were fascinated with the writings.

Interestingly, according to Hindu Yogis, the vibrational impulse of Laghimā (Becoming Lighter), that was a particular aspect of the Siddhiḥ (Achievements), ensured the individual could become weightless and rise in the airspace. Hence, the vibrational waveforms enable Humans to effectively levitate. The uniquely designed Vimanas had some kind of Central Computer System (CCS) that could absorb the psychically emitted thought waves of the navigator. Those individuals who piloted the Vimanas used a psychically formatted console to steer the aircraft with quickened ease. This meant the Artificial Intelligence was derived from the interaction of the navigator with the internal metallic structure of the aircraft. A film that can explain this type of Artificial Intelligence the 1986 movie called Flight Of The Navigator, that was directed by John Randal Kleiser.

After 10 years of research which the U.S. Defense Department funded at Purdue University, which is located in West Lafayette, the Synthetic Environment for Analysis and Simulations (SEAS) technologies were achieved on the 2006. What became known as the Sentient World Simulation (SWS) was established as the ultimate objective of the Synthetic Environment for Analysis and Simulations (SEAS), which the U.S. Defense Department uses to collect users data from the Internet. Alongside this, paranormal activities have become very prevalent in the city of West Lafayette, and have been present in the Wabash Township of Tippecanoe County, as with other areas within Indiana and the wider Midwestern United States, for thousands of years. Does the Sentient World Simulation (SWS) have any connections with the etheric lifeforms who create the paranormal activity? Because the Sentient World Simulation is supposed to be a digitally based duplication which correlates with the 3D Holographic Reality of this Material Dimension, maybe the Military Industrial Complex (MIC) has also considered the idea of duplicating the numerous dimensions which resonate beyond spacetime. The notable researcher called Professor Seth Lloyd, who is employed at the Massachusetts Institute of Technology (MIT), has suggested that the entire Physical Universe could be simulated by using qubits or quantum bits, that are the basic information units of quantum computing. Therefore, from knowing this, it becomes clear that Artificial Intelligence could be used to access such faster vibration dimensions.

Along with this, it is believed the Sentient World Simulation not only receives data from the Internet, but also from smartdust, even though such an idea sounds like a subject from a science fiction movie that Hollywood would produce. But the usage of smartdust is very real, and is a technical process that involves the usage of numerous tiny Micro Electro-Mechanical Systems (MEMS) which include sensors, robots and other devices. The purpose of using these methods is to detect luminescence, temperature, vibration, magnetism and chemicals. Hence, it is possible that smartdust has already been place into the environment across Canada and the United States of America. Does this mean track and trace has already been activated?

The Sentient World Simulation has been created as the method which can be used to duplicate the Divine Creation of the Universal Creator. Because this digital process has not been designed to assist Planet Earth, but to replicate the condensed vibrations which defines the 3D Holographic Reality of this Material Dimension, this would suggest this confirms the Elites actually worship Lucifer. Another reason that the Sentient World Simulation has been developed is to make Humans fully dependent on their own subjective beliefs and perceptions across every location across Planet Earth, so the individual thoughts of Humans can then be contained in the biodigital convergence of the New World Order (NWO). Both Artificial Intelligence and the Sentient World Simulation could actually benefit the spiritual development of Humans, if these scientific processes were not intended to be used as methods to restrict and manipulate the perceptions and thoughts of Humans. Therefore, such Occult Technology is used by the Elites and their Secret Societies, to prevent us from knowing who we truly are during our incarnations.

According to the famous theoretical physicist Doctor Geordie Rose, who is the cofounder of D-Wave Systems. This company manufactures these kinds of quantum computing machines, which can even tap into parallel dimensions. He also stated that Earth Humans need to watch out for an overflow of "Demons" or "Aliens" which reside in the Infernal Region of the Astral Plane. With the use of Artificial Intelligence, the hordes of Demons can therefore gain etheric access to Planet Earth. Doctor Geordie Rose said that the D-Wave Quantum Supercomputers are able to summon etheric lifeforms that are similar to *"Demons*" or "*Aliens*" and have qualities that make them equivalent to the Great Old Ones spoken of by the famous American Horror Novelist called Howard Phillips Lovecraft, in his shared fictional setting of the Cthulhu Mythos. Doctor Geordie Rose actually made the following statement about this situation:

"This Things We Are Summoning Into The World Now Are Not Demons, Not Evil But More Like The

Lovecraftian Great Old Ones, They Are Entities Not Necessarily Going To Be Aligned With What We Want." Doctor Geordie Rose also mentioned that if Humans *"Are Not Careful"* then Artificial Intelligence (AI) could *"Wipe Us All Out."*

Additionally, Doctor Geordie Rose stated that standing next to one of these D-Wave Quantum Supercomputers is like standing at the *"Altar Of An Alien God."* So this kind of statement clearly indicates that many of the Elites and their Secret Societies, intend to use the development of D-Wave Quantum Supercomputers, for contacting etheric lifeforms which exist within the Infernal Regions of the Lower Astral.

The subterranean device called the Large Hadron Collider (LHC) was constructed near to the city of Geneva, in the Geneva Canton of South Western Switzerland, but extends beneath the Annemasse Commune of the Haute Savoie Department, in the Auvergne Rhône Alpes Region of Eastern France as well. The advanced Large Hadron Collider (LHC) is the biggest and highest of its kind on Planet Earth. Besides the publicly announced there are theories that these huge electromagnetic systems are used for Parallel Dimensions, Parallel Realities and Parallel Universes, and the access the Astral Plane. Different interfaces have been produced so that Artificial Intelligence can link with the frequencies and vibrations. When researched, you will find this links to the Saturn Cube, which is actually the Saturn Hexagon, and the Moon Matrix, which together work as a tuning fork, keeping us in this vibration. The prudent Elites and their Secret Societies obviously want to subvert the very fabric of spacetime, and summon Demons from the Infernal Regions of the Lower Astral.

With Elon Reeve Musk having become the rebel he seems to be, the business magnate stated during the 24 October 2014 "*With Artificial Intelligence, We Are Summoning The Demon,*" at the Centennial Symposium of the MIT Aeronautics and Astronautics Department. Elon Musk statement about Artificial Intelligence, needs to be considered:

"*You Know All Those Stories Where There's The Guy With The Pentagram And The Holy Water And He's Like, Yeah, He's Sure He Can Control The Demon, But It Doesn't Work Out.*"

The 51 Qubit Quantum Supercomputer has been developed, and many Quantum Supercomputers have been seemingly produced to resonate with demonic frequencies. By using the D-Wave Quantum Supercomputers, computations can be sped up, as the D-Wave Quantum Supercomputers can directly resonate into an unimaginably vast fabric of the 3D Holographic Reality and the Astral Plane, that is counter intuitive to quantum mechanics.

There is a connection in Artificial Intelligence to aspects of Ceremonial Magic, Western Occultism, Eastern Occultism and Witchcraft. Coding has become the 21st Century Wizardry, being able to control the masses through programming algorithms. Even a form of warfare. If someone wanted to control Human Consciousness, they would want to understand the how the Divine Creation emanates from the Universal Creator. Or even replicate the frequencies and vibrations that define the 3D Holographic Reality of the Material Dimension.

Although the essence of Artificial Intelligence is neither good or evil, the individuals who maintain and develop them, are very distorted in their thinking. There is certainly a dark side to Artificial Intelligence. Was there a reason why the book Childhoods End has never been made into a film? When Sir Arthur Charles Clarke wrote Childhoods End in 1953. he was obviously trying to convey some kind of message about Ultraterrestrials and Extraterrestrials. However, if this Artificial Intelligence is understood it could positively resolve many issues on Planet Earth, such as poverty and sickness. Hence, the Artificial Intelligence could be implemented to bring about an Earthly Kingdom and not a synthetic prison.

We are at a significant juncture on Planet Earth and therefore Humans are now in a situation where they will have to make an important choice. Every aspect which defines Artificial Intelligence only has the volition that we actually give to it. Therefore, we must remember that as Humans we have so much potential, because of the emotions and thoughts which define us as sentient existences.

CHAPTER 13: THE SPIRITUAL BATTLES

We are certainly in a etheric conflict where the vibrational polarities of good and evil are obviously present on Planet Earth, because the consistent suppression and censorship is intended to manipulate the beliefs and thoughts of Humans. Just beyond the electromagnetic parameters which define the 3D Holographic of this Material Dimension are malevolent lifeforms who know that much of the historical truth about Planet Earth has to be repeatedly concealed from the public. Hence, we are here to learn about the vibrational opposites of good and evil, and the censorship of the past, so we can spiritually develop ourselves.

The eminent Irish American Traditionalist Catholic Priest, archaeologist, Exorcist, Palaeography Professor and Jesuit Priest called Malachi Brendan Martin, who also used the pseudonym of Michael Serafian, was trained to be an Exorcist by the Roman Catholic Church (RCC) at the Vatican City State.

Malachi Brendan Martin wrote *Hostage To The Devil: The Possession And Exorcism Of Five Living Americans* (1976), which gives testimonies about demoniacs from the United States, who he spiritually healed. When he became the Palaeography Professor at the Pontifical Biblical Institute, on the 18 April 1962, Malachi Brendan Martin was able to study historic writing structures that included Hebrew and Aramaic. By doing this he then found out more about how civilisations dealt with the Devil and the Demons.

Another individual who helped numerous afflicted demoniacs was an Italian Catholic Priest and the supervisor of Papal Exorcists in the Status Civitatis Vaticanae (Prophecy City State), Father Gabriele Amorth. Whilst he was at the Vatican City State in Rome, he became the most famous Catholic Exorcist on Planet Earth. Father Gabriele Amorth wrote *An Exorcist Tells His Story* (1999) and *An Exorcist: More Stories* (2002), which describe his memoirs and experiences of dealing with those who were demoniacs. The important 84 page document called '*Of Exorcisms And Certain Supplications*' was used by Father Gabriele Amorth and others in the Roman Catholic Church (RCC), and it contains the current version of the Rite of Exorcism which designated Catholic Exorcists have to use to effectively heal those who have become demoniacs. Many individuals would visit him from all over Planet Earth to ask for help in defeating the malicious influences of Satan and his Demons. Hence, there were numerous individuals who reached out to Father Gabriele Amorth so they could defend themselves against the Devil who uses intrapsychic subversion to manipulate the minds of susceptible Humans.

The word 'Daemon' originates from the Greek Language and denotes a Spirit or inverted Divine Power, much like the Latin word 'Genius', which is defined as some kind of 'Spirit' or 'Numen.' The word 'Daimon' most likely came from the Greek Language verb 'Daiesthai,' that means to 'Divide' and 'Distribute.' The actual Greek Language terms do not actually initially have any connotations of evil or malevolence. By the time of the Early Roman Empire, cult statues were seen by the Pagans and the Christians, as objects that were inhabited by the ethereal presence of the Astral Deities, whether they were benevolent or malevolent. Like the Pagans, many of the European Christians sensed and perceived the Astral Deities and their potency. Hence, over many years, a collective shift occurred, and many of the Astral Deities, which may well have been Demons that had disguised themselves, had done so to deceive the minds of Humans. Because of this, many individuals turned the concept of the Daimones into existences that were malevolent Demons, who served the instructions and plans of Satan, who is also called the Devil. Additionally, there is the Luciferian Consciousness, which emerged as the spiritual development of Humans can only happen if they can truly sense what good is because a contrast arises from the frequencies of evil. Hence, the energetic inversions known as Demonic Oppression and Demonic Possession, are important as they methods by which Humans can learn about good. Far beyond spacetime, there are swarms of Demons who inhabit the reaches in the Infernal Region of the Lower Astral, which apparently is where the Fallen Angel known as Lucifer, also resides with absolute dominance.

According to Catholic Theology, there are four stages of malevolent progression that occur before a Demon can entirely manipulate the thoughts and emotions of a Human, and these are Temptation, Infestation, Oppression and Possession. Within the doctrines of Christianity, and especially Catholic Theology, stories of how the Devil and his Demons like to subvert the minds of Humans, is consistently presented. Many individuals know that the Devil and his Demons like to use intrapsychic messages, which they maliciously transmit from the Infernal Region of the Lower Astral, so as to tempt Humans into focusing on committing sinful transgressions, which includes deception, accusation, doubt, seduction, and provocation. These kinds of messages are intended to cause emotional and psychological disturbances in the minds of Humans, even though most Humans no longer believe the Devil and his Demons exist and therefore ignored the subject of evil. Because the logical precepts of Western Science have been used to rationalise away the existence of malevolence and the concepts of Lucifer and Satan, this has allowed the Demons which reside in the Infernal Region of the Lower Astral to increasingly take over the minds of Humans without most afflicted individuals having any kind of awareness that certain thoughts might not be their own.

Much of Biblical Christianity reveals how the cardinal sins, which are likewise called sinful transgressions, are enticements which Humans need to resolve and prevent during their incarnations on Planet Earth. There are many sinful transgressions and these include pride, greed, anger, envy, sexual desire, gluttony, and laziness, which is comprised of spiritual, physical and mental lethargy. Even if the scientific rationalists in Mainland Europe and North America wish to no longer believe in the existence of Lucifer and Satan, this does not mean that evil itself can be ignored, because the vibrations of evil resonate beyond spacetime from within the Infernal Region of the Lower Astral. From inside the murky fiery reaches of that etheric location are vast multitudes of Demons, which have always been devoid of any love or empathy towards any lifeforms in the 3D Holographic Reality of this Material Dimension.

Another stage of malevolent progression is called Infestation, which concerns those Demons which make unusual noises in houses and other buildings. The noises tend to have no logical source. Such creepy kinds of Demons can sometimes pinch, scratch or pull the hair of the afflicted. There are occasions when these kinds of Demons appear in the peripheral vision of Humans, where they are seen to briefly move from right to left, which is unlike the motions of Angels, which involve them moving in any direction.

Whenever an Infestation occurs, the activity is usually heightened during the nighttime. Sometimes the Demons who create the Infestations can take on the form of anyone, which means they can even impersonate very young infants. The subject of Demons is something that may seem like just another facet of World Folklore, but such lifeforms truly do exist, and when it comes to the process called Oppression, the swarms of Demons, will use both Internal Oppression and External Oppression. From what we know, the first version concerns the intrapsychic communication that a Demon will try to use so it can maliciously influence the thoughts of a vulnerable Human. Many professional Exorcists believe that once an individual begins to identify with the disturbing thoughts in their minds, it can then cause serious long term psychiatric issues. Whilst this continues to happen, the Demon will command the individual it has been harassing, by committing malevolent acts. Sometimes the individual will feel intense rage and not know why they do. Many of those Humans who feel Oppression emanating from a Demon, will also have vivid nightmares or wake up during the night and even observe the outlines of a darkened figure in their peripheral vision.

The energetic process of External Oppression involves the Demon consistently trying to limit and restrict the hope and prospects of an individual. Hence, the Demon can subversively create many loud noises that are very audible to help with distracting and disrupting the minds of the afflicted. For example, the Demon might decide to create a sound of a siren or even thunder. But when the individual checks to see whether the sounds are real or not, there is nothing there. Other forms of evil that are expressions of the External Oppression include the situation when a Demon started to move, throw or turn furniture upside down.

Finally, the Demon will try and use Possession, by entering the aura of an individual, which ensures the afflicted individual will then start to exhibit augmented strength, voice changes, and their eyes will become darker and glazy looking. The objective of the Demon is usually to cause emotional and physical harm to the relatives and friends of the person who has become maliciously controlled.

We have been given many astounding insights about the Angels, from the religions of Judaism, Christianity and Islam. From beyond spacetime, the choirs of Angels resonate with the glory of the Universal Creator. Indeed, the Angels collective name is a description of their official status, and not a name which describes their actual existences. The religions of Judaism, Christianity and Islam mention the Archangels, which in the Hebrew Language are defined as the Rukhot Koranot (Radiant Spirits) and the Shlikhim Elohayim (Divine Envoys). Each of the Archangels have the supremely fast vibratory rates and emit distinctly coloured luminescent wavelengths. Hence, the benevolence of the Archangels meant each of them became named as Michael, Gabriel, Raphael and Uriel. They consistently observe the evil of the Devil and the Demons, by watching how they cause problems for Humans. Because good can only become apparent if we can sense that evil is a tangible resonance, this means the Demons are in effect an important aspect in our spiritual development.

In the Holy Bible, there are some fantastic insights which is given in the Book of Ephesians, that explains the importance of good and evil:

"Put On The Whole Armour Of God, That Ye May Be Able To Stand Against The Wiles Of The Devil. For We Wrestle Not Against Flesh And Blood, But Against Principalities, Against Powers, Against The Rulers Of The Darkness Of This World, Against Spiritual Wickedness In High Places." (Ephesians 6:11-6:12).

Another quote from the Holy Bible, that reveals the profound relevance of the supernal contrast that arises from the vibrations of good and evil, is written in the Book of Revelation, where it clearly indicates how serious the problem of evil truly is on Planet Earth:

"And The Great Dragon Was Cast Out, That Old Serpent, Called The Devil, And Satan, Which Deceiveth The Whole World: He Was Cast Out Into The Earth, And His Angels Were Cast Out With Him." (Revelation 12:9).

The renowned Dominican Friar and Catholic Priest, Tommaso D'Aquino, who is more commonly known as Saint Thomas Aquinas says in his *Summa Theologica: Tractatus De Angelis (Summary Of Theology: Treatise On The Angels)*, that there must be purely supernal lifeforms and that the Universal Creator produces creatures by his intellect and will. Therefore, *"The Perfection Of The Universe Requires That There Should Be Intellectual Creatures."* (I.50.1, I.14.8, I.19.4).

Saint Thomas Aquinas also says that the minds of Angels are higher than the minds of Humans because intellect is above the learning and cognition of Humans, which means the Angels use a superluminal kind of perceptivity. The famous American Philosopher known as Professor Peter John Kreeft provides one possible explanation in his book *Angels And Demons: What Do We Really Know About Them?* (1995), describing how Angels communicate with each other.

The choirs of Angels instantly communicate from a single thought, which each of them shares with immediate discernment. In others, the choirs of Angels use superluminal telepathy, which they brightly transmit from beyond spacetime, across Celestial Hyperspace and into the Heavenly Kingdom.

Over the expanse of boundless epochs, the conflict between Angels and Demons has always been an interdimensional psychic offensive, where the etheric intellects of both the Angels and Demons confront each other, and the electromagnetic differences produce intensely contrasted vibrations which further define good and evil. Hence, the conflict between the Angels and Demons is effectively conveyed as waveform patterns of electrons, which move with superluminal instancy. The legendary Hindu Indian Ascetic called Paramahansa Yogananda, wrote *Autobiography Of A Yogi*. He made numerous profound statements concerning benevolence and malevolence, such as *"Good And Evil Must Ever Be Compliments On This Earth"* and *"There Can Be No Images Of Light Without Contrasting Shadows. Unless Evil Had Been Created, Man Would Not Know The Opposite, Good."*

In the book called *The Physics Of Angels: Exploring The Realm Where Science And Spirit Meet*, that was written by Timothy James Fox, who uses the pseudonym of Matthew Fox, and Alfred Rupert Sheldrake, mention how the choirs of Angels are shimmering agents who continually intercede for Humans, whenever an individual sincerely reaches out for supernal help. Sometimes the Angels will guard, defend, inspire us and announce changes. Additionally, the choirs of Angels heal us, and sometimes they can usher Humans into other dimensional locations, from which it becomes possible for us to perceive the 3D Holographic Reality of this Material Dimension with a completely different perspective. Hence, the Angels call upon Humans to become focused on their own spiritual development and make proactive improvements.

Every single Angel is a hyperspatial Theío Pnéuma, Θείο Πνεύμα (Divine Spirit), which means the Angels do not have discernible vibratory outlines, and therefore are not comprised of any condensed waveforms. From the perspective of vibratory expression, each of the Angels has individual traits and volition, and from within Celestial Hyperspace and the Heavenly Kingdom, the choirs of Angels are often sent by the Universal Creator to carry out specific duties on Planet Earth. Hence, this is why the word 'Angel' when translated, means 'Envoy' and 'Messenger.'

Because alien abductions have occurred for many years on Planet Earth, the contingents of Reptoids and Orion Grays who have taken Humans onboard their spacecraft, have sometimes been prevented by the Angels which have travelled from Celestial Hyperspace and the Heavenly Kingdom, to intervene and prevent such events from occurring. When the alien abductions happen, teams of Zeta Reticulan Type A Grays and Zeta Reticulan Type B Grays, have also been apparently stopped by intervening Angels. From knowing this, we need to consider whether the Reptoids and Grays have vibrational connections with Demons. After the Greada

Treaty was established on the 20 February 1954, various kinds of alien abductions began to happen. From this date and onwards, numerous alien abductions started to occur in Canada, and the United States of America. Other similar kinds of alien abductions likewise began to occur in Mexico, Guatemala, Belize, Honduras, Nicaragua, Costa Rica, Panama, Venezuela, Columbia, Ecuador, Peru and Brazil. Even though such interactions occurred, many of the alien abductions were prevented by the intercedence of Angels, who neutralised and destroyed the Reptoids, Orion Grays and Zeta Reticulan Type A Grays and Zeta Reticulan Type B Grays. Were alien abductions originally intended to become a vibrational part of the spiritual development which Humans need to resolve their emotional and psychological issues whilst they exist on Planet Earth?

CHAPTER 14: ASTRAL PROJECTION

The concept of Astral Projection is a fascinating subject, that has become another example of an Out of Body Experience (OBE). Essentially, the etheric action of using Astral Projection occurs when an individual who exists in the 3D Holographic Reality of this Material Dimension, shifts the vibratory rate of their Astral Body, so they can leave their corporeal self behind for a temporary duration. Although this incredible etheric process has not been validated by academics, the Central Intelligence Agency (CIA) and other related organisations from the United States Intelligence Community are very well known for the extensive levels of scientific studies they have done to confirm the validity of Astral Projection. Numerous individuals have been trained by the CIA to use effective Astral Projection, so they can effectively navigate in the 4D Holographic Reality of the Astral Plane.

Around 15 percent of individuals regularly experience Astral Projection. This means that such individuals are able to view different geographic locations around the Planet Earth, and sometimes they are able to explore other planets and moons in the Solar System, from unusual views, perspectives or angles. This means that more than 1 in 10 individuals experience Astral Projection, even though such an etheric process is unconsciously activated.

Much of Western Science currently defines Astral Projection as some kind of pseudoscience, because academics in the Republic of Ireland, the United Kingdom, Mainland Europe and North America, believe the laws of physics cannot be applied to the etheric processes of Astral Projection. However, millions of

Humans around Planet Earth continue to experience Astral Projection, which is an event which has regularly occurred since their childhoods. Additionally, there are many accounts where clients who have had regressive hypnotherapy sessions, describe the 4D Holographic Reality of the Astral Plane.

The covert etheric data gathering program that became known as the Stargate Project began on the 15 April 1972, at the Stanford Research Institute in Menlo Park, Northern California. During the 23 June 1978, the Stargate Project was initiated at Fort Meade in Central Maryland. Because the Defense Information School, and the Defense Media Activity, are located at Fort Meade, this indicates how important the Stargate Project actually was. Additionally, the United States Army Field Band, and the headquarters of the United States Cyber Command are situated at the same facility. Because the National Security Agency (NSA), the Defense Courier Service, the Defense Information Systems Agency (DISA) and the Cryptologic Warfare Group 6 of the U.S. Navy, are likewise situated at Fort Meade, this further emphasises how important that facility was for the advancement of the Stargate Project for the U.S. Federal Government.

Once the Stargate Project began on the 23 June 1978 at Fort Meade, Maryland, the Defense Intelligence Agency (DIA) and SRI International, which originated at the Stanford Research Institute, then commenced with carrying out numerous scientific studies into the viability of Astral Projection and Scientific Remote Viewing (SRV). The Stargate Project was a 20 million U.S. Dollar program, that was developed, so that Intelligence Officers could find the most effective method for moving Human Consciousness beyond spacetime, so that remote data gathering could be accomplished. Hence, to achieve this objective the CIA employed psychics who became definable Scientific Remote Viewers. The individual known as Ingo Douglas Swann was a psychic, spiritual artist, and profound writer from the United States of America, who helped to create the process of Scientific Remote Viewing (SRV), along with Russell Targ and Harold Ernest Puthoff. Every aspect of the etheric techniques which Ingo Douglas Swann, Russell Targ and Harold Ernest Puthoff had cleverly developed, became the overt basis of the Stargate Project.

During the 18 February 1975 the renowned psychic called Ingo Douglas Swann was contacted by an individual from the U.S. Defense Department and Military Industrial Complex (MIC) in Washington DC. It was an Intelligence Officer from the Defense Intelligence Agency, who had phoned him from the Defense Intelligence Analysis Center (DIAC) in the premises of Joint Base Anacostia-Bolling (JBAB) at Washington DC. The Intelligence Officer guardedly advised Ingo Douglas Swann that he would soon be receiving a telephone call from a Jewish American known as Colonel Gershom Shachna Axelrod or Mister Axelrod, who appeared to be from Marine Corps Intelligence (MCI). Although Ingo Douglas Swann also believed that Mister Axelrod was working alongside the CIA. The source of Ingo Douglas Swann quietly advised him that while he could not offer much at that time by way of a meaningful explanation, but the Intelligence Officer did say that he should be keenly aware that the phone call from Mister Axelrod would concern a matter of immense urgency and importance.

When Ingo Swann wrote his autobiography, called *Penetration: The Question Of Extraterrestrial And*

Human Telepathy (1998), he stated that *"People Fill In The Unknown With What Fits With Their Known."* Hence, this indicated how some Humans tend to filter their own awareness levels. After some emphasis had been given to the huge metallic looking citadel which soared upwards from the surface of the Moon, Ingo Swann realised these were structures that no Humans could have built. With intense brevity Mister Axelrod told Ingo Swann that Ultraterrestrials or Extraterrestrials had constructed the buildings on the Moon.

Additionally, further rostered Scientific Remote Viewing revealed to Ingo Swann how the bizarre topography of the Moon conceals a wealth of domed crystalline structures, advanced machinery, glinting metallic towers, large cross structures and tubular constructions across the landscape. During these sessions, Ingo Swann also observed what appeared to be extensive mining operations. Apparently, certain kinds of Ultraterrestrials or Extraterrestrials had secretly constructed nothing less than a subterranean base on the Moon. Over subsequent covert sessions Ingo Swann observed gatherings of Humanoids who appeared to be housed in some kind of metallic enclosure on the Moon, that were very busily excavating and burrowing into the side of a cliff.

The concept of Astral Projection is concerned with moving the Astral Body beyond spacetime to create a form of perspective awareness, whilst the concept of Scientific Remote Viewing involves moving Human Consciousness beyond spacetime. There is nothing mysterious about either Astral Projection or Scientific Remote Viewing. Because the United States Senate and United States House of Representatives funded the

Stargate Project, this confirms that such an etheric data gathering program really did exist.

Every scientific and logistical aspect of the Stargate Project was designated to Detachment G of the United States Army Intelligence and Security Command (INSCOM) and eventually became a very important scientific program of the U.S. Army. When the Stargate Project was established on the 23 June 1978 at Fort Meade, Maryland, by the Defense Intelligence Agency (DIA) and a contractor from Stanford Research Institute, known as SRI International, it was intended to equivalently oppose the Soviet Union which had already developed extremely advanced knowledge concerning Astral Projection and Scientific Remote Viewing (SRV). Some indication of the knowledge the Soviet Russians had covertly gained, is extensively given some explanation in the book called *Psychic Discoveries Behind The Iron Curtain* which Sheila Ostrander and Lynn Schroeder wrote and published in 1970.

Some of the reasons why psychic abilities were perceived to be important, specifically concerned the establishment of the internecine Glavnoje Upravlenije Generalnogo Shtaba Vooruzhonnykh Sil Rossiyskoy Federatsyi (Main Directorate Of The General Staff Of The Armed Forces Of The Russian Federation), that was formerly called the Glavnoye Razvedyvatelnoye Upravleniye, GRU (Main Intelligence Directorate, MID). This part of the Soviet Government was established on the 16th February 1942, and various sorts of psychic abilities were then intrinsically studied. Additionally, the same reasoning was used when the Komitet Gosudarstvennoy Bezopasnosti (Committee For State Security) or the KGB, was created on the 13 March 1954.

When the lady known as Ninel Mikhaylova, who became known as Ninel Sergeyevna Kulagina, was found to be a psychic, she became the subject of ongoing scientific studies by the Main Intelligence Directorate (MID) and the Committee For State Security or KGB, whilst she resided in Saint Petersburg and elsewhere in the North Western Federal District of Soviet Russia. Her psychic abilities were observed from the 20 June 1943 to the 26 April 1987, in Saint Petersburg, and in the towns of Gatchina, in the Gatchinsky District, and Lomonosov, in the Petrodvortsovy District. The parapsychologist and physiologist from Soviet Russia, who was called Leonid Leonidovich Vasiliev, carried out scientific studies on the psychic abilities of Ninel Mikhaylova, for the General Secretary of the Communist Party of the Soviet Union, called Ioseb Besarionis Dze Jughashvili, who most know as Joseph Vissarionovich Stalin or Josef Stalin.

To divert attention away from the real scientific studies the Soviet Union was actually doing, they established the Institut Zadacha Informatsyi Peredachi (Institute of Problems of Information Transmission), on the 30 September 1948. Everything about this parapsychology facility in Moscow, was intended to function as a diversion. To help create an impression of authenticity, the Soviet Russians made sure the Institute of Problems of Information Transmission was protected at all times. As for the real scientific studies, they were carried out in a massive facility named Akademgorodok (Learning Town) or Naukograd (Science City), that was established on the 12 April 1957. This vast facility is located midst the Sovetsky District of Novosibirsk, in the Siberian Federal District of Central Russia.

One of its scientific facilities was called the Institut Avtomatiki I Elektrometryi (Institute for Automation and Electrometry). From the 12 April 1957 and onward, Special Department 8 was designated in that premises. Nobody could gain entry to the premises of Special Department 8 unless they had access to an encrypted code, that was changed on a weekly basis. For the 63 academics employed at Special Department 8, their specific tasks involved the investigation of telepathy and distant influence, which otherwise became defined as Biokommunikatsyi (Biocommunication) or Zhiznkommunikatsyi (Biocommunication).

Another profound researcher who was known as Professor Ivan Maksimovich Mikhailov, was employed in the Akademiya Nauk Sovetskogo Soyuza (Academy Of Sciences Of The Soviet Union). Once that learning facility was founded on the 27 July 1925 in Moscow, he began to carry out extensive studies into Extra Sensory Perception (ESP) for the Soviet Union. These studies lasted from the 23 June 1958 to the 11 October 1968. The famous academic from the Soviet Union, known as Valery Grigoryevich Petukhov, who claimed to be the Senior Technician of the Biophysics Laboratory at the Gosudarstvennogo Kontrolya Institut Mediko-Biologicheskikh Issledovaniy (State Control Institute of Medical and Biological Research), did some profound scientific studies into the viability of Astral Projection and Extra Sensory Perception (ESP). Much of these studies were privately done in a facility that was situated in Moscow, and urban areas like Belgorod, in the Central Federal District of Western Russia.

One of the many programmes that emerged from the Stargate Project, was the experiment that became known as the Mars Exploration, which occurred during the 22 May 1984. Where Joseph McMoneagle, who is more commonly known as Joe McMoneagle, a retired U.S. Army Chief Warrant Officer, who covertly worked as Remote Viewer Number 1, with U.S. Army Intelligence, the Stanford Research Institute (SRI) and the Defense Intelligence Agency (DIA). Claimed he observed huge five sided pyramids, a massive obelisk structure and huge road networks on the surface of the Planet Mars. The timeline for the Scientific Remote Viewing (SRV) session was 1,000,000 BC, according to the documents which the CIA recorded during the experiment known as Mars Exploration.

Joseph McMoneagle claimed he left the Stargate Project during December 1984 with a Legion of Merit Award. This was for providing information on over 100 targets from information that could only be obtained by using Scientific Remote Viewing (SRV). He served in 450 missions between June 1978 and December 1984, where he also helped to located hostages and the Red Brigades. Joseph McMoneagle became a training instructor at the consciousness development facility known as The Monroe Institute, that was created by Robert Allan Monroe, who is now retired.

Robert Monroe was a radio broadcasting executive who became famous as a researcher into altered states of consciousness. He founded the Monroe Institute during the 14 October 1985. The Monroe Institute teaches individuals to effectively use Scientific Remote Viewing (SRV). Whilst he experienced his first Out of Body Experience on the 23 October 1958, Robert Allan Monroe apparently observed himself. He is also credited for inventing the term '*Out Of Body Experience.*' Robert Monroe wrote some profound books about Astral Travel, and these were *Journeys Out Of The Body* (1971), *Far*

Journeys (1985) and *Ultimate Journey* (1994). According to Robert Allan Monroe the more spiritually aware Humans know they are here on Planet Earth to further learn about their own incarnations:

"Advanced Souls Know That They Cannot Change The System And They Don't Wish To. They Are Content To Enjoy Themselves In The Earth Life System And The Only Influence They Exert Is To Maximize Their Experience."

It is very common for individuals who have been involved with traumatic incidents, to have a Near Death Experience (NDE), which for them became an intensely profound version of Astral Projection. Where a person observes the traumatic incident or has some kind of accident, they are given the vibrational opportunity to spiritually develop. Sometimes they will perceive themselves in a hospital whilst such individuals are hovering in the 4D Holographic Reality of the Astral Plane. Many accounts have been given, concerning a situation where an individual perceives themselves lying on a sanitised table in an operating theatre, during surgery, it becomes a profound supernal observation for them. Sometimes the individuals who have had the Out of Body Experience, remember conversations which medical staff were having during the surgical procedure.

Within the Vedic Indian Scripture called the Māṇḍūkya Upaniṣad (Spiritual Anguish Secret Doctrine), the concept of Chatūriya, Tūriya, Chatūrtha, which means 'The Fourth,' that defines pure though in the Human Mind, is given tremendous emphasis, as the meditative process allows the individual to navigate beyond spacetime. Apparently, Chatūriya, Tūriya, Chatūrtha, are the frequencies pervades the three common states of

Human Consciousness, which are the waking state, the dreaming state and the dreamless deep sleep. During the the Belle Époque (Beautiful Time Fixture) of the Third French Republic, this meditative routine was known as Clairvoyance Itinérante (Travelling Clear Vision) and during the Victorian Period of the United Kingdom, this process was also called Telethēsía, Τελεσθησία (Distance Wanting Sensations), in spiritual circles. The supposed response to or perception of distant stimuli by means of Extra Sensory Perception (ESP).

For many generations the American Indian Tribes have spiritually honoured the incredible knowledge of the renowned Ojibway Indian Astral Guides called Wabanquot Bagakasige (White Cloud Shines Brightly) and Nawakamig Zagaaso (Midst The Universe Center Radiates Forth), by using Astral Projection to meet with them. Additionally, other profound individuals who reside in the 4D Holographic Reality of the Astral Plane, are known to be the Cherokee Indian Astral Guides who are called Degataga Juhyvidlvi (Standing North) and Onacona Ganohilvisv (White Hooter Flying). Such incarnations regularly communicate with Cherokee Indians and other receptive individuals from the American Indian Tribes.

With this, many Humans who unconsciously like to leave Planet Earth by using Astral Projection, will sometimes encounter one of the Ascended Masters and communicate with them by using telepathy, whilst they explore the 4D Holographic Reality of the Astral Plane. Within that luminescent etheric location, the Ascended Masters such as Maitreya Chamakal, Sanat Kumara, Maurya Bhavyan, Kuthumi Pavitaraika, and Count Saint Germain, whose real name is Master Rakoczy Lelkiegy, exist in piety and blissful reflection. Other individuals sometimes communicate from the resonant vibrations in the 4D Holographic Reality of the Astral Plane, with the four Archangels known as Michael, Gabriel, Raphael and Uriel, who resonate beyond spacetime in Celestial Hyperspace and the Heavenly Kingdom.

The famous psychic and healer known as Edgar Cayce, was from Hopkinsville in South Eastern Kentucky and Selma in South Central Alabama. Edgar Cayce would regularly claim he could receive messages from his Higher Self, whilst he was in a trance-like state. Many of his patients called Edgar Cayce the Sleeping Prophet. Edgar Cayce did 1,200 readings on Egypt, where he revealed the origin, purpose and prophecies of the Great Pyramid and the Sphinx, mystically controlled rulers, and his own past life as the Temple Priest called Ra-Ta, who wanted to unify the spiritual teachings of Human Beings.

The famous Serbian inventor called Nikola Tesla developed many dreamscape experiments. With his acute, hearing, and visualisation skills, Nikola Tesla allowed him effectively use complex visualisations, where he connected himself into a lucid state beyond the 3D Holographic Reality of this Material Dimension. Was Nikola Tesla able to focus his thoughts upon another frequencies? When you look into his work, you realise how advanced it was and therefore what has happened to the scientific discoveries Nikola Tesla left behind? His inventions can never be forgotten.

Every aspect of Western Science has constructed its own walls of academic restriction and can never explain such frequencies, and therefore any reasoning about the concept of Astral Travel or Scientific Remote Viewing is dismissed. However, beyond spacetime, the frequencies of the Astral Plane resonate next to the 3D Holographic Reality of this Material Dimension.

But as the CIA described in their own documents *"The Discovery Of The Energy Underlying Telepathic Communications Will Be The Equivalent To The Discovery Of Atomic Energy."* Even if this is the case, substantial amounts of damage could occur, if such knowledge was gained by the wrong kind of individuals.

Most individuals do not need any kind of scientific proof that Astral Projection or other kinds of psychic phenomenon are real, because such experiences are intuitively centred within the minds of the experiencer, who do not look to Western Science for confirmation that Astral Projection or Scientific Remote Viewing are real. Hence, the overwhelming evidence which has been gathered from the numerous accounts of Astral Projection and Scientific Remote Viewing, simply cannot be ignored.

So without any doubt whatsoever, Humans have an Astral Body, and a higher state of intense spiritual awareness. However, we allow ourselves to become trapped in egocentric thinking and overwhelmed by the mundane routines that we have become so familiar with. Do the Elites and their Secret Societies perceive the dimensional reaches beyond Planet Earth to be a threat? From gaining a discernment about the Astral Worlds, it becomes obvious as to why Humans are not taught about this in schools, colleges and universities. Maybe it is the case that individuals need to understand the malevolence which opposes the Human Soul, as such vibrations function as the contrast which individuals need to spiritually develop their own true selves. We can use these experiences to improve our minds and to inspire others. Because each of us has chosen to incarnate on Planet Earth, we are meant to fearlessly resolve the challenges of existing here, and learn about this kind of fascinating information.

Printed in Great Britain
by Amazon